The People of God

Also by Dom Anscar Vonier
Published by Assumption Press

The Human Soul and its Relations with Other Spirits

The Personality of Christ

A Key to the Doctrine of the Eucharist

The Christian Mind

The Divine Motherhood

The Life of the World to Come

The Art of Christ: Retreat Conferences

The Angels

Death and Judgement

The New and Eternal Covenant

Christ the King of Glory

Christianus

The Victory of Christ

The Spirit and the Bride

Sketches and Studies in Theology

The People of God

Dom Anscar Vonier
Abbot of Buckfast

2014

✠ Nihil Obstat.
Reginaldus Phillips, S.Th.L.,
Censor Deputatus.

✠ Imprimatur.
L. Can. Evans,
Vicarius Generalis.

Westminster
April 21, 1937

The *Nihil Obstat* and *Imprimatur* are official declarations that a book or pamphlet is free of doctrinal or moral error. No implication is contained therein that those who have granted the *Nihil Obstat* and the *Imprimatur* agree with the content, opinions or statements expressed.

Copyright © 2013 Assumption Press. This material may not be reproduced, displayed, modified or distributed without the express prior written permission of the copyright holder.

This book was originally published in 1937 by Burns, Oates, and Washbourne.

Cover image: *Mosaic of the Loaves and Fishes,* at the Church of the Multiplication, Tabgha, 4th Century

Contents

Preface
i

Introduction
1

ONE
The Ideals
7

TWO
The Ancient People
12

THREE
The Concept of "People of God" in Christianity
21

FOUR
The Heart of the People of God
29

FIVE
The Shepherd and King
38

SIX
The Rights of the People of God
45

SEVEN
The King and Reaper
50

EIGHT
The Activities of the People of God
60

NINE
God's Patience with His People
69

TEN
The Religion of the People of God
76

ELEVEN
The Divine Latitudes
84

TWELVE
The Divine Interventions
89

THIRTEEN
The Supplications of
the People of God
95

FOURTEEN
The Popular Aspect of the Divine Gifts
105

FIFTEEN
The People of God and the Altar
117

SIXTEEN
The Consecration of the People
125

Conclusion
131

The People of God

✠

Preface

With the furious assaults on religion by the powers of evil, the temptation may come to the pious to retire into a sort of spiritual solitude because they despair of the victory of organized Christianity. Each soul for itself, they seem to say, a united front is no longer possible on the part of believers.

The following simple pages are written on purpose to combat this not uncommon temptation. Instead of faltering we ought to feel more and more deeply our spiritual solidarity as one "people of God." This short book is chiefly exhortatory for the hour of tribulation, so it has no pretensions to exhaust so vast a subject. When writing of the "people of God," the whole range of supernatural life could be touched upon, as it would be appropriate and congenial to the matter. To do this would necessarily mean producing an immense treatise on Christian virtues; but such an effort would obscure the principal issue of the subject. So I shall confine myself to what will be mere sketches of the salient features of the theme. The end I have in view is to add my voice to many others, immensely more powerful, to rally Catholics into a fervent realization of their corporate existence.

Anscar Vonier, O.S.B., *Abbot*.
Buckfast, Easter, 1937

Introduction

IN THIS BOOK IT IS MY INTENTION TO EXPLAIN THE spiritual possibilities contained in the one term "people of God." This appellation is not only frequent in Christian literature, it is directly scriptural; in fact, in the Scriptures of the New Testament it is used as often as the word "Church," while it fills every page of the Old Testament. The titles "people of God" and "Church" stand, of course, for the same objective reality—the believers in Christ considered as a unit. The appellations are co-extensive in their meaning. But this need not prevent our finding a definite form of spiritual instruction in the very circumstance that the Christians are a "people of God" as well as a "Church." They are a "Church" which is also a "people of God," or if we like to take it the other way, they are a "people" endowed with the dignity of a "Church." The two notions supplement each other and help us to form a more complete conception of the nature of the assembly of Christ's faithful.

The utterances concerning the Church in the New Testament are comparatively few, but they are immensely pregnant with meaning.

Catholic theology, on the other hand, has expanded the idea of the Church with inexhaustible activity and has made of the doctrine of the Church a most superb monument of sanctified thought. The notion "people of God" is also generously treated in the New Testament, though not in the Gospels, for reasons to which I shall return. But the whole Old Testament is an endless presentment of the idea of a people of God, at least in an adumbrated and prophetic sense.

Catholic theology, however, has not developed this concept as it has developed the concept "Church." The reason is to be found, I think, in this, that by *Ecclesia* the newness of the second dispensation and its profound originality as a divine institution is more forcibly brought home. We know that the Church means a plenitude of supernatural graces, an entirely divine institution, a creation of the Holy Spirit, a fullness of charismata; such features are not commonly associated with the word "people." On the other hand, the acts of divine providence, the deeds of God's mercy and justice, the varieties of human powers and merits, the tribulations and successes of life, the external works of religion and many other things of which we shall speak, denote more directly the ways of a people.

The same persons are, as already insinuated, the members of the Church and of the people and this in virtue of the same supernatural election through faith. But I think that our understanding of the mystery of Christ's Church ought not to make us overlook all the possibilities contained in the repeated declarations of the inspired Word that we are the "people of God." Much is to be learned from this proclamation by God's messengers and there is a certain narrowness of treatment of the doctrine of the Church which is not an uncommon danger even for the theologian; his concept of the Church imperceptibly becomes too mystical and too internal. This narrow-

INTRODUCTION

ness is precisely corrected if we associate considerations concerning the "people of God" with the dogmas of the Church of Christ.

I do not pretend to say that it is possible to compose a thesis on the "people of God" with the same exactness which is to be found in the theological treatises on the Church; but as we possess the whole ancient Testament to draw from, it seems certain that there can be created a very strong external atmosphere in which the theology of the Church ought to move. Let us call it the popular atmosphere. By this we intend to convey that, lofty and holy as the Church is, she is still a people's Church. A "people" is not defined by spiritual categories, but if it can be defined at all it is made clear through its classes of high and low, of rich and poor, of strong and weak, of sinner and just man. Let us say, moreover, that the notion of "people" adds to the notion "Church" in a permanent and irrefragable fashion the characteristic of externalness. If we consider the Church to be a people we are certainly saved from the danger of all those tendencies which seek to make of the Church an invisible society of saints and elect.

It is, then, in this sense that the following pages are written. It is my most ardent wish to make Catholics understand how manifold, how rich is their life in Christ; how they constitute in this world a great new society of whose existence the powers of evil are extremely jealous. Anticipating already some of the considerations that will occur in this book, may we not say that two great assaults have been made on the fortunes of Christendom? Protestantism set out, unconsciously perhaps, to strip Christianity of the glory of being a Church, one, undivided, holy Church; the movements, on the other hand, to which we give the generic name of "modern revolution" have made it their task to deprive Christianity of being a "people" in this world. There may be individual Christians, says the revolutionary of all hues, but they must not be a Christian society, a form of policy which takes its cue from the Gospel; he does not want a "people of God"; nationhood must be entirely secularized.

It would be too presumptuous to say that these modest pages are written against modern revolution; they are written for Catholics themselves, so that they be renewed in that happiness which ought to be theirs because they are truly God's people.

The notion "people" is, of course, closely allied to that other concept "kingdom." In Scriptural thought and phraseology the two words are interchangeable. This was true in the ancient dispensation even before there were kings in Israel, as Jehovah Himself was always the one true King. The relationship between the earthly king of Israel and his people is expressed in the homage offered to David:

> Then all the tribes of Israel came to David in Hebron, saying: Behold we are thy bone and thy flesh (2 Kings 5:1).

It would seem then that the consecrated terms of the New Testament "kingdom of heaven" and "kingdom of God" stand for the same reality conveyed by "people of heaven" and "people of God." Both "people" and "kingdom" are ideas that are final, whereas Church is an idea that may be called covenanted, in the sense that it stands for the dispensation that is to sanctify the people, that is to build up the kingdom. It is to be taken for granted that the kingdom of God, the mention of which fills the Gospels, is not different from the Church, from the whole divine institution which is the work of Christ. The Gospel of the kingdom is simply Christ's Gospel as He delivered it, as it was confirmed by the Holy Ghost at Pentecost. Says Aquinas, "It would be silly to say that the Gospel of Christ and the Gospel of the

INTRODUCTION

kingdom of God are not the same thing."[1]

Comparing these three divine realities, "people of God," "kingdom of God," and "Church," we can only pretend to approach one and the same fundamental thing from three different angles; there can only be a diversity of emphasis in stating the same truth.

Let us then put it tentatively in the following way. When we say "people of God" we have before our eyes a multitude of human beings, extremely diverse in endowments, very active, carrying out the spiritual warfare, all of them possessing one common supernatural life, acknowledging one leader. When we say "kingdom of God" or "kingdom of heaven," we think more of the providential arrangements made for that people, of the heavenly inheritance, of the splendor of setting and the wealth of grace divinely prepared for that people; the security of the dispensation and its transcendence over all human contingencies. When, finally, we say "Church," we lay stress on the great power of sanctification, on the union of all the members with Christ their Head, on the operation of the sacramental institutions, on grace and the charismata of the Holy Spirit. But when all has been said, it is the one sanctified human multitude, redeemed by the Son of God and chosen by Him out of the world, that is at the same time "people of God," "kingdom of God," and "Church of God."

It may be asked why it is that all theology concerning the corporate life of the believers in Christ under the new dispensation is the theology of the Church, not the theology of the "people of God" or of the "kingdom of heaven." This is particularly striking when we compare the number of times the kingdom of God is spoken of in the Gos-

---

1 St. Thomas Aquinas, *Summa Theologiae,* II, q. 106, a. 4, ad 4: "Stultissimum est dicere quod Evangelium Christi non sit Evangelium regni."

pels with the single mention of the Church. "Kingdom of God" and "kingdom of heaven" and "Gospel of the kingdom" occur more than a hundred times, "Church" only once. We know that all the attributes of the Church are also the attributes of the "people" and of the "kingdom." I think we might look for the reason of this preference precisely to that particular sentiment awakened in us by what we read concerning the Church in the New Testament. It stands there as an unsurpassable power of sanctification, as a pillar and column of truth, as a continuation of Christ's Person, as an organism vivified by the Paraclete. These aspects are directly the sources of light for Catholic theology which is chiefly concerned with the ways of man's salvation.

There is also this feature which the three great realities here described have in common: "people of God," "kingdom of God" and "Church" have all three a double aspect, the terrestrial and the celestial; the period of combat and the eternity of glory. The Fathers, but chiefly St. Augustine, abound in this wisdom. They see clearly how one and the same institution, without changing its substantial character, is spoken of in divine Writ, now as struggling upon this earth, now as spotless and glorious in heaven. The "people of God," the "kingdom of God" and the "Church" have this quality of oneness of essence under a twofold external manifestation. The eternal life that constitutes them in their basic elements is the same life in time and in eternity; but the external setting of that life is diverse, according as it is either the struggle in this world or the triumph in the world to come.

The "people of God" then, to make use of another metaphor expressing corporate human vitality, is an army which today is fighting on the battle-fields of this earth and tomorrow will enter triumphantly into the city of God. From this point of view there is complete identity between the three aspects of the society of Christians.

✠ 1 ✠

The Ideals

Any Christian with the love of God in his heart is capable of drawing in his mind a picture of the people of God; he need only remember what God is, as far as it is possible in this life to possess a notion of the divine Majesty. A people of God, then, would be one for whom God is the supreme interest, the ultimate value, the beginning and the end of all undertakings, the final arbiter of all issues, the uncontested policy; so that men would live for Him without any reservation. It does not matter whether such a people be in heaven or on earth, whether it see God face to face or in the twilight of faith; the behaviour is identical. All works, all thoughts are for God. Men would start enterprises for God whether they received His orders through the intermediary of a prophet or in the clear communication of heavenly light; the obedience, the singleness of purpose and the zeal of action would be the same.

Such a people, then, would sing the praises of God whether employed in ploughing the fields for the harvests on this planet or contemplating the Divinity in the unrevealed splendor of eternity. Its members would beget children here on earth with as much sanctity of intention as they would associate with the high spirits who do not possess flesh and blood. They would praise God with the instruments of the material world as joyfully as with the intellectual comprehension of the mysteries of eternity. The great and the small would praise Him. If necessary they would fight the enemies of God, they would wield weapons with as much singleness of purpose as they would sing the canticles of peace in the kingdom of the Father. Nothing would come amiss to such a people. They would see God in everything, they would act for God in everything, they would expect everything from God.

It would not be against this ideal view of the people of God that they should be made to undergo hardships, if this were necessary for the glorification of God; for it would be evident that labors and travail would have an essentially transient character and that all suffering would end in a warmer welcome on the part of God to His returning soldiers. A permanent state of unhappiness, however, or of endless physical suffering would be contrary to the ideal of a people of God, because it is not thinkable that happiness should be perpetually absent from such a people.

The relationship between God and His people has infinite possibilities. The terms King, Sovereign, Lord, Father, could all be pressed into service without exhausting the nature of that relationship. In fact no human term exists that could adequately represent the position of God in the midst of His people. Ultimately there is only one expression that would be satisfying, that God should say to His people, "I am your God." This would not only mean every kind of beneficent relationship known to man but something more, because to be God to any one is a unique privilege and an infinite contact. It would signify not only ruling but also vivifying: it would be the brightness of sunshine, the beauty of creation, the sweetness of love, the harmonies of music, the tenderness of compassion, the patience of friendship; God would be all that to His people inexhaustibly, to an infinite degree.

By the very fact of being the people of God men would find themselves as it were, in a beautiful climate, in a paradise of delight, in a place of security. One belonging to the people of God would be safe and protected wherever he went, carrying in himself the marks of the divine citizenship. No enemy could hurt him, no evil could overcome him. The saying of Christ that the Father would send twelve legions of angels if they were necessary for protection would be applicable to the smallest child belonging to the people of God, for we could not imagine God being the Sovereign over His people on any other terms.

The people of God would be an amiable people, possessing the ways and the manners that come from intercourse with Majesty; they would not necessarily be sinless but at all times ready for repentance, so that any sin that might be committed would be the matter of sorrow and contrition, the occasion of greater fidelity. Unrepentance would be antagonistic to the character of such a people, not transient sin. A state of sinlessness may be granted by God to His people as the reward of repentance, but it is not essential to the idea of a people of God. If there is sin in that people, through a just dispensation on the part of God, there is also affliction as a rectification of the claims of sanctity; and it will be the talent of the people of God to see the wisdom and the justice of that affliction, to bear it with patience, in a spirit of humility. By doing this they will show themselves eminently to be God's own people, for thus they admit the claims of His justice and submit themselves to Him as to the supreme Judge.

We show our loyalty to our natural nationhood by accepting the judicial authorities of the ruling power; much more do we prove ourselves to be God's own people when we proclaim the justice of His judgement, when we submit to His punishments. So a people actually the prisoners of God's justice would not in the least cease to be His people: if they rebelled, if they blasphemed, then they would be not only strangers but outcasts. We could quite well imagine God addressing a multitude of suffering beings in terms of endearment and Calling them "My people" though they were all under duress, if their state of sorrow and affliction were a punishment accepted with resignation for offences committed against Him. That such is the case we know from the Church's teaching concerning those spirits that are in prison, the souls of the elect that are purified before being admitted to eternal bliss. No multitude of creatures more deservedly possesses the title of people of God than those spirits, though their existence be in bitterness.

The conviction that they form one people would of necessity breed amongst the men comprehended under that title a fellowship quite unique in the experience of mankind. Wherever they meet they know each other to be fighting under one King, to be obeying one Master, to have at heart the interests of one Sovereign. This sentiment of the radical oneness of their race would save them from such dissensions as would be fatal to the existence of a people. It is not part of a people's constitution to have absolute uniformity of life; variety is not only a sign of health but its very condition. A people of God would abhor instinctively a sameness of mind and sentiment which would deprive it of all vital initiative; every sort of diversity in the gifts possessed by the people is necessary in order to bring about wealth in thought, in love, in action.

But this very multiplicity of endowments will constitute the one intrinsic danger for the people's existence: division of ideals, opposition of interests. From this danger the people will be saved by an intensive sentiment of brotherhood, by an instinctive appreciation of vital issues, by a clear understanding that everything has to yield in the last instance to the advantage of the community. The intercourse, therefore, of such a people with each other will have the charms of a heavenly society even here on earth; their bond of union will be their love of their Sovereign. There will be no contempt of any man, because his divine nationhood makes of him a true nobleman; mercy and kindliness, forbearance and patience, a love of the lowly and a sincere compassion for all sufferers will, of course, be the most evident traits in the character of the people of God.

✠ 2 ✠

The Ancient People

There is a doctrine of the people of God as there is a theology of the Church. For the Christian dispensation, we consider that the theology of the Church covers the whole field of man's covenanted relationship with God. There is no theology of the synagogue—the synagogue and the Church are opposite concepts—but there is the theology of the people of God, covering the whole field of God's covenanted relationship with man before Christ. What I mean to say is this: up to the coming of Christ there is a dispensation of a most definite character, and that dispensation ought to be called the dispensation of the people of God. The ancient covenant in a most unmistakable fashion is God's relationship with a people. So one is justified in saying that whatever theology belongs to the old law is the theology of a people.

Whatever spiritual favors, whatever temporal privileges the Jewish race enjoyed, it all comes under this one heading, that they were the people of God. So in very truth this great title belongs to the province of theology. The Jewish infant entered into supernatural life through its membership with the people of God.

We may ask ourselves the question how the infants of the Jewish race were given sanctifying grace. When we think of the great saints of the Old Law we are naturally tempted to enquire how their souls first became united with God, how, for instance, did St. Joseph find grace and justification? The answer to all such queries is technically theological but happily very simple: becoming members of the race through circumcision they were added to the people of God and as such were sanctified in their souls.

Fortunately nothing is more abundant than the witness to the great truth that the Jewish race were made the people of God. In fact, there is no religious truth of any time that has been announced with greater solemnity nor been repeated with greater emphasis. Every page of the Old Testament is a proclamation of it, and unless we reject the divine character of the Bible we have to admit that over no matter has God been so explicit as He has been over this one point. It is, of course, to be remembered that when God chose His people He had in view the final development which St. Paul expresses so eloquently in the Epistle to the Romans. Of that people "is Christ according to the flesh, who is over all things, God blessed forever. Amen" (Rom 9:5). This ultimate destiny puts all things in due proportion and we cannot be surprised that so much is revealed to us concerning God's dealing with His people, concerning the nature of that wonderful nationhood.

There can be no mistaking the meaning of God's intention when for the first time He makes it clear that the descendants of Abraham would be made into His people. This divine proclamation was made at a definite date, under historic circumstances quite peculiar and strongly characterized. The twelve sons of Jacob had grown into an immense multitude in the land of Egypt; they were a race, but they were not an independent people; for all practical purposes they were the slaves of Pharaoh. It is those unorganized multitudes who will receive, at a given hour, a definite political status, directly from God, so that they will be no longer the servants of Pharaoh but the people of God:

> I have heard the groaning of the children of Israel, Wherewith the Egyptians have oppressed them: and I have remembered my covenant. Therefore say to the children of Israel: I am the Lord who will bring you out from the work prison of the Egyptians; and will deliver you from bondage, and redeem you with a high arm, and great judgements. And I will take you to myself for my people. I will be your God: and you shall know that I am the Lord your God, who brought you out from the work prison of Egypt, and brought you into the land concerning which I lifted up my hand to give it to Abraham, Isaac, and Jacob. And I will give it to you to possess. I am the Lord (Exod 6:5-8).

This message of Jehovah to Moses is truly the constitution of the people of God; therefore it is the first time the term "my people" is used by God. The contrast between their condition of bondage and their future liberty leaves no doubt as to the meaning of this new compact: they are a people of slaves; presently they will be the people of God. Jehovah puts all His power into the execution of this tremendous political upheaval: "With a high arm and great judgement" will He begin His sovereignty. This sovereignty is dated from the Exodus, the going out of the children of Israel from Egypt. Before that date the Scriptures use the word "friend" in speaking of God's faithful servants; no group of men is called the people of God. Scripturally the expression is as exclusive and as technical as it possibly could be. After that date, for a thousand years and more, the title "people of God" fills the inspired literature of the Jewish nation. Very soon, when the history of the Jewish race begins its long course with the first days of its independence in the wilderness, the Lord speaks of the political status of God's people as an accomplished fact:

> But I say to you: Possess their land which I will give you for an inheritance, a land flowing with milk and honey. I am the Lord your God, who have separated you from other people … You shall be holy unto me, because I the Lord am holy: and I have separated you from other people, that you should be mine (Lev 20:24, 26).

Moses, who is not the king of that people but its temporal leader, comes back unceasingly to this fundamental principle—the election of Israel:

> But the Lord hath taken you and brought you out of the iron furnace of Egypt, to make you his people of inheritance, as it is this present day (Deut 4:20).

> Because thou art a holy people to the Lord thy God. The Lord thy God hath chosen thee, to be his peculiar people of all peoples that are upon the earth. Not because you surpass all nations in number, is the Lord joined unto you, and hath chosen you: for you are the fewest of any people. But because the Lord hath loved you, and hath kept his oath, which he swore to your fathers: and hath brought you out with a strong hand, and redeemed you from the house of bondage, out of the hand of Pharaoh the king of Egypt (Deut 7:6-8).

The word commonly employed in order to describe this dispensation is the term "theocracy." To the modern ear it is only a variant of autocracy, democracy, plutocracy, it has no longer a pleasing sound. Revolutions in modern times have pretended to be the enemies of all theocracy, as if it were some extremely black form of tyranny. It is, of course, to be admitted without any hesitation that the Jewish polity was a theocracy, a people governed by God, a nation radically bound to God as their Sovereign. It is not my intention to present the reader with an anthology of inspired texts proclaiming this theocratic nationhood; what is the reading of the ancient Testament but all unceasing reminder of the truth of the words which God spoke to Moses in Egypt?

The attempt has been made in our own days to write the history of the Jewish people in an entirely natural fashion, leaving aside completely the element of theocracy. It has been claimed that one can give a satisfactory interpretation of the vicissitudes of the history of the Jewish people through the ordinary laws of critical history, through the political actions and reactions inside and outside Palestine. Thus where the Bible says that Jehovah in His anger will deliver His people into captivity, the historian is able to show how this captivity was a natural consequence of political forces, and that there is nothing more theocratic in the political misfortunes of the Jewish people than in the defeats and downfalls of other kingdoms of the same period.

The Catholic dogmatic standpoint does not in the least ask of us to see in the fortunes of the Jewish people anything miraculous except in a few instances whose supernatural character is made evident by the context. There was nothing miraculous in all that befell that people when, at a later period, it was placed between the rival ambitions of Babylon and Egypt, of the powers that were on the

Euphrates and those that resided on the banks of the Nile. But this by no means interferes with the reality of the theocracy. God makes use of human events for His own purposes; it was in His power to save His people and it was in His power to let His people fall into the hands of its enemies. Right through the history of Israel theocracy is proclaimed as a force that can preserve a nation from its enemies and as an authority that may let the enemy loose on a sinning people:

> But for the wrath of the enemies I have deferred it: lest perhaps their enemies might be proud, and should say: Our mighty hand, and not the Lord, hath done all these things. They are a nation without counsel and without wisdom. O that they would be wise and would understand, and would provide for their last end! How should one pursue after a thousand, and two chase ten thousand? Was it not, because their God had sold them, and the Lord had shut them up (Deut 32:27-30)?

> If my people had heard me, if Israel had walked in my ways: I should soon have humbled their enemies, and laid my hand on them that troubled them (Ps 80:14-15).

Theocracy does not create the political situation, it utilizes it. The Bible is the reading of the history of the Jewish people from God's point of view. The strictly miraculous events are few and far between, the Exodus being, of course, the greatest of them; but the fewness of those directly divine interventions is no argument against the totality of the theocracy; the human events are entirely in the hands of God and all we need believe in order to preserve the character of the ancient theocracy is this control by God over the deeds of peoples.

We do not in the least deny that it is possible to write a tolerably connected history of Israel in the same strain as one would write of the Egyptians, but the fact remains that of all the ancient nations, Israel alone survives to this day; how can we explain this amazing survival by merely natural causes?

Among the innumerable pronouncements of the Spirit concerning the people of God there is hardly one that is more characteristic than the vaticination of Ezekiel over the dry bones of the house of Israel. We may quote it here for its finality and its splendor of utterance. The prophet had been shown the vision of many bones lying out on the face of the plain, and they were exceeding dry. And he was ordered by the Lord to prophesy and then sinews and flesh came up to them and the skin was stretched out upon them and the Spirit came into them and they stood upon their feet, an exceeding great army:

> And he said to me: Son of man: All these bones are the house of Israel. They say: Our bones are dried up and our hope is lost and we are cut off. Therefore prophesy and say to them: Thus saith the Lord God: Behold I will open your graves and will bring you out of your sepulchers, O my people, and will bring you into the land of Israel. And you shall know that I am the Lord: when I shall have opened your sepulchers and shall have brought you out of your graves, O my people, and shall have put my spirit in you. And you shall live and I shall make you rest upon your own land. And you shall know that I the Lord have spoken and done it, saith the Lord God (Ezek 37:11-14).

At the time of this prophecy the people of God was dispersed, the Jewish nation had apparently come to an end. The metaphor of the dry bones being made to live again expresses the unchangeableness of God's counsel, even with the skeleton of Israel there remained the Covenant of God; the people had been brought to the verge of annihilation, yet God never allowed its complete disappearance. Even the "plain full of bones" (Ezek 37:1) was something tangible, the bones had not as yet fallen into dust, they were hard and solid. With the prophesying of Ezekiel, with the coming of the Spirit, in a moment there stood up a living, political organism, the Jewish people after their captivity.

We know that this prophecy has a further meaning: the reconstruction of the people of God in the highest sense, the resurrection of the just at the end of the world. More than any other divine utterance, the prophecy of Ezekiel brings home to us the varieties of vicissitude that may befall the people of God in their long history. At one time it, may seem that the people were right in saying, "Our bones are dried up and our hope is lost and we are cut off," but this is merely an appearance; the breath of life is never far, the identity of the people is never interrupted.

This is the special lesson and instruction conveyed to us by the notion of a "people." We are enabled through that notion to see in a more satisfying proportion the succession of prosperity and failure in the assembly of those who are God's own. A people can stand practically any misfortunes, it is a unit even under the most distressing misfortunes, it can be brought to the verge of extinction and is still a people.

It has often been a matter of wonder how very little concerning the spiritual destiny of individuals is to be found in the Old Testament; it has even been hinted that there are no clear indications in the Old Testament concerning individual immortality. It is, of course, abundantly evident that the Bible is essentially the book of a people not the chronicle of individual men. In it a whole nation is being educated and instructed. Men are taught to behave as the members of a people. In this the Old and New Testaments are at one; for this reason the inspired books are irreplaceable. It is their very characteristic to be social in outlook; they never contain anything which is not a norm for the whole multitude of the elect of God.

✠ 3 ✠

The Concept of "People of God" in Christianity

THE BEGINNINGS OF THE NEW TESTAMENT ARE STILL couched in terms of the theology of the people of God. The angel announces to Zachariah that the son whose birth he promises will "prepare unto the Lord a perfect people" (Luke 1:17), and when the tongue of the old priest is loosened he sings of the people's new privilege, "Blessed be the Lord God of Israel: because he hath visited and wrought the redemption of his people" (Luke 1:68). The Virgin Mother glorifies God because "He hath received Israel his servant, being mindful of his mercy" (Luke 1:54).

The Messiah comes to the old people of God, He is their expectation: the theology of the people of God is an integral part of the theology of the Incarnation. After the coming down of the Holy Ghost, Paul, full of the Spirit, preaches the continuance of the divine dispensation; the God of the people of Israel is also the God of the new grace:

> The God of the people of Israel chose our fathers and exalted the people when they were sojourners in the land of Egypt: and with an high arm brought them out from thence (Acts 13:17).

After having considered thus the far-reaching and all-embracing significance of the concept of people in the Old Testament and on the threshold of the New, we have to ask ourselves whether this notion has been carried over into Christianity in its entirety or left behind as no longer expressing the completeness of the relationship between God and man. Is the notion of a people of God an imperfect institution like the observance of the Law of Moses, or is it, on the contrary, a thing of everlasting value, not to be superseded by anything new in Christianity but only to receive, if necessary, in Christianity greater splendor and profounder meaning?

It is certain that in the Psalms and the Prophets the expression "people of God" has already the sound of a universal truth, nothing could be greater in mankind than the existence of such a people. In the Gospels this great title never occurs for reasons which we shall expose in another chapter. Christ's terms for stating the new order of things are only three: the "kingdom of God," the "kingdom of heaven," and the "Church"; the word "people" He never uses even in a parable when He wants to give utterance to the new state of things. To express universal evil the word "world" is invariably His chosen term, and for the universality of good the "kingdom of God" and the "kingdom of heaven" are titles that fill the Gospels. The term "Church" occurs once, but with such significance that no one can be mistaken as to its importance:

> And I say to thee: That thou art Peter, and upon this rock I will build my church. And the gates of hell shall not prevail against it (Matt 16:18).

What then had become of that glorious old title, the "people of God?" That very notion was as much alive in the Jewish people then as it had ever been. Was the Greek word λάος (*laos*), people, to be expunged forever from New Testament nomenclature, so that there was no more a people? Here we come upon a spiritual element of the first order in Christology. Far from there being a rejection of the notion that there is a people of God, the title has been transferred, with all the solemnity of a juridical act, from the Jewish nation to the Christian believers. There is certainly the new people of God. God has not rejected this title. God has not been tired of having a people, as if His experience in the past had been too discouraging. There is now a people of God more truly and more completely than there ever was.

This is the theology of St. Paul in the Epistle to the Romans. After Christ's ascension to heaven the Apostles were free to proclaim without fear to the world the existence of the people of God, and they did so with a truly Jewish enthusiasm. There are the Christian souls:

> The vessels of mercy which he hath prepared unto glory. Even us, whom also he hath called, not only of the Jews but also of the Gentiles (Rom 9:23-24).

These men are the people of God, and in order to prove this St. Paul recalls the prophecy of Hosea:

> I will call that which was not my people, my people; and her that was not beloved, beloved; and her that had not obtained mercy, one that hath obtained mercy. And it shall be, in the place where it was said to them: You are not my people; there they shall be called the sons of the living God (Rom 9:25-26).

The title has been transferred. In doing this God acted justly: "Hath not the potter power over the clay" (Rom 9:21). But what about that long association between God and the Jewish nation, are they no longer His people?

> I say then: Hath God cast away his people? God forbid ! For I also am an Israelite of the seed of Abraham, of the tribe of Benjamin. God hath not cast away his people which he foreknew (Rom 9:1-2)...

The Apostle lays it down as an absolute ruling that the "gifts and calling of God are without repentance" (Rom 9:29). So persevering is the relationship between God and those whom once He considered His people that even in the case of Israel all obstacles will ultimately yield to the supreme reality that Israel is His people. As a people they will come back to God:

> For I would not have you ignorant, brethren, of this mystery (lest you should be wise in your own conceits) that blindness in part has happened in Israel, until the fullness of the Gentiles should come in. And so all Israel should be saved, as it is written: There shall come out of Zion, he that shall deliver, and shall turn away ungodliness from Jacob (Rom 9:25-26).

Nothing could show us more clearly than the superb argumentation of St. Paul concerning the rejection and the reconciliation of the Jewish people, how great a role the notion of people played in the mind of that great expositor of the grace of Christ; in fact, one may doubt whether St. Paul ever viewed Christianity otherwise than in the light of the people of God. To create unto Himself a new people is, according to St. Paul, the end of the Incarnation. His magnificent passage merits to be quoted in its entirety:

> For the grace of God our Savior hath appeared to all men: Instructing us, that, denying ungodliness and Worldly desires, we should live soberly and justly and godly in this World, looking for the blessed hope and coming of the glory of the great God and our Savior Jesus Christ. Who gave himself for us, that he might redeem us from all iniquity and might cleanse to himself a people acceptable, a pursuer of good works (Titus 2:11-14).

The denomination "acceptable people" is an institutional expression going right through the Scriptures; a people is essentially a worker, a conqueror; the people of God, in the grace of the Savior, is a "pursuer of good works"; no people ever had a more comprehensive mission.

St. Peter likewise emphasizes the transference of the glorious title of people to the Christians of all nations, "Who in time past were not a people: but are now the people of God" (1 Pet 2:10). The majestic words of that first ruler of the Christian people are in the ears of every one of us: "You are a chosen generation, a kingly priesthood, a holy nation, a purchased people" (2 Pet 2:9).

The Apostles had been familiarized from their childhood with the patriotic songs and solemn canticles of the Scriptures which declared in every variety of language that they were the chosen people of God. Without hesitation, now that the Lord is in the glory of the Father, they ask the Christian neophytes to make their own the utterances of Moses and the prophets; more than ever is there on earth a people of God, exalted above all other nations. Their supernatural nationhood has precisely this characteristic, to make them a class of men completely and radically different from other men. The distinction, in St. Paul's forcible language, is as between light and darkness:

Bear not the yoke with unbelievers. For what participation hath justice with injustice? Or what fellowship hath light with darkness? And what concord hath Christ with Belial? Or what part hath the faithful with the unbeliever? And what agreement hath the temple of God with idols? For you are the temple of the living God; as God saith: I will dwell in them and walk among them. And I will be their God: and they shall be my people (2 Cor 6:14-16).

In the Epistle to the Hebrews this juridical transference of nationhood is the leading theme of that matchless tract of theology:

For this is the testament which I will make unto the house of Israel after those days, saith the Lord: I will give my laws into their mind: and in their heart will I write them. And I will be their God: and they shall be my people (Heb 8:10).

The day of rest, σαβατισμός (*sabbatismos*), which the ancient people did not enjoy, is the privilege of the new people of God: "There remaineth therefore a day of rest for the people of God" (Heb 4:9). A new order of things has arisen, a new creation has been accomplished and a new people, the Christian people, are the beneficiaries of the work which Christ has achieved: we are in full possession of all the works of God.

In St. John's Revelations, the people of God are exhorted to separate themselves from all the nations and the kings of the earth who have drunk of the wine of Babylon and have been corrupted by her:

And I heard another voice from heaven, saying: Go out from her, my people; that you be not partakers of her sins and that you receive not of her plagues (Rev 18:4).

The consummation of the mystery of God is again a proclamation of the supernatural nation:

> And I heard a great voice from the throne, saying: Behold the tabernacle of God with men: and he will dwell with them. And they shall be his people: and God himself with them shall be their God (Rev 11:3).

There can be no doubt then that the concept "people" applied to the Christian community is apostolic and comes from the Spirit of Pentecost. We may take it for granted that the early Christians had a clear consciousness of their privilege, that they knew that in a higher degree they carried on all the dignity and all the burden that had been laid on the shoulders of the ancient people of God.

In a general way the drama of the Apocalypse is more the drama of a people than of a Church; the battle between good and evil is the life of a people, the history of a nation. It is true that the great metaphor of the Bride comes periodic ally like a culmination of the fight between the Lamb and the Beast, but the fight itself is not only that of a Bride, but equally that of a people; the Bride is triumphant; the people is at times triumphant but at times it is overcome by the Beast who has received power to overcome the saints, who are the people of God.

Already in the oracles of the prophets God passes from the denomination of "people" to that of a woman whose fidelity He expects; in divine language the transition from the "people of God" to the Bride of the Lamb is natural. Yet, for our more complete understanding of God's relationship with those who are baptized in Christ it is as necessary to think of them as a people as it is consoling to think of them as a Church or as the Bride of the Lamb. The vicissitudes of Christianity, its triumphs and its failures, its endless varieties of gifts and opportunities, its position in the world, its contact with the human race, are best under stood if we know Christians to be the "people of God."

✠ 4 ✠

The Heart of the People of God

There is in Holy Writ an amazing insistence on the nature of the spiritual phenomenon that will be the making of the new and true people of God. A change of heart, on a scale that is no longer human, will come over men, and by that change of heart a new people will be created. The prophets foretell, with great emphasis of language, that hearts of flesh will succeed to hearts of stone, or more properly, to no hearts at all, and the new people will be to the old what flesh is to a stone; they will be a people through all the innermost laws of life.

The nationhood which will be the crowning work of God's power will have this in common with every genuine nationhood in nature, it will have the cry of flesh and blood. Men and Women will belong to it through the subtlest nerves of their being and there will be a loyalty that is entirely spontaneous and quite irresistible in its main line of force. There will be no element of coercion in the assembling of the new people. Men will not belong to it against their will, they will not feel conquered and subjugated against their stronger aspirations by a mightier power. There will not be the least *residuum* of rancor against anyone, but they will glory in their name of "people of God" unreservedly, whole-heartedly, with all the enthusiasm and spontaneity of a youthful and entrancing life.

The experience of history teaches us how long-lived national rancors may be; how lasting may be the memory of wrongs suffered by those who were brought under the sway of a political power by a deed of violence. Centuries-old grievances may flare up into terrific conflagrations, because in spite of superficial appearances, there never was a true fusion of wills in the conquests of many years ago. The wrong done then has left its ineffaceable scar. As for the men who are actually brought under the domination of a hostile power by force of firms, their hearts remain stony in their attitude towards that power and the conquest is nothing else than a physical coercion. Nothing is more difficult than to make one race out of divergent and opposing elements. Men will feel strangers to each other during many generations before the fusion of sentiments is complete.

Now the Scripture most clearly proclaims the fact that in the new people of God there will be none of that reluctance, none of that inhibition, none of those rancors, but whole-heartedly, with unreserved enthusiasm, with fervent love, that people will accept its nationhood, will welcome its liege Lord, the God of Glory.

By all we can gather from the utterance of the Holy Ghost in the Scriptures, we are made to see in the people of God a nation of fervent patriots. No one will be in that people against his choice, no one will regret another allegiance from which he himself or his father before him has been torn against his desire.

The people of God about which we write is, indeed, an apparition in human history so unique, nay, even so strange, that we are fully justified in pondering carefully over the burning phrases in which the prophets announce the coming of that people. In it, loyalty to God will be, so to speak, an atavistic element. No one will be able to explain its presence except on the assumption that God Himself is present, deep down in the psychology of that people.

The great prophecies which foretell this divine atavism of attachment to God come from the Seers who were the witnesses of the apostasies of Israel of old. The vision of the new people is by way of contrast; the Jews fall away from Jehovah as a stone tower sinks to the ground when its foundations are undermined: they were of stone and as stones they are scattered. The sight of this collapse is most dismal indeed. Never again will Jehovah build Himself a house of stone; He is resolved to erect for Himself a dwelling of living palpitating human hearts:

> Thus saith the Lord God: I will gather you from among the peoples and assemble you out of the countries wherein you are scattered and I will give you the land of Israel. And they shall go in thither and shall take away all the scandals and all the abominations thereof from thence. And I will give them one heart and will put a new spirit in their bowels: and I will take away the stony heart out of their flesh and will give them a heart of flesh: That they may walk in my commandments and keep my judgements and do them: and that they may be my people and I may be their God (Ezek 11:17-20).

> And I will give you a new heart and put a new spirit within you: and I will take away the stony heart out of your flesh and will give you a heart of flesh. And I will put my spirit in the midst of you: and I will cause you to walk in my commandments and

to keep my judgements and do them. And you shall dwell in the land which I gave to your fathers: and you shall be my people and I will be your God (Ezek 36:26-28).

Behold the days shall come, saith the Lord, and I will make a new covenant with the house of Israel and with the house of Judah: Not according to the covenant which I made with their fathers, in the day that I took them by the hand to bring them out of the land of Egypt: the covenant which they made void, and I had dominion over them, saith the Lord. But this shall be the covenant that I will make with the house of Israel after those days, saith the Lord: I will give my law in their bowels and I will write it in their heart: and I will be their God and they shall be my people. And they shall teach no more every man his neighbor, and every man his brother, saying: Know the Lord. For all shall know me from the least of them even to the greatest, saith the Lord (Jer 31:31-34).

We are made certain, from the utterances of the New Testament, that Jeremiah and Ezekiel saw the new people of God when they thus vaticinated. In the Epistle to the Hebrews, St. Paul simply copies the words of Jeremiah to bring home his great contention that a more excellent order of things had been established by the coming of Christ. Again in the Apostle's rich and varied metaphor that the Christians are a letter written by Christ, the supreme character of a spiritual idiosyncrasy in the faithful is brought out:

You are the epistle of Christ, ministered by us and written: not with ink but with the Spirit of the living God: not in tables of stone but in the fleshly tables of the heart (2 Cor 3:3).

St. Paul adds the words, "And such confidence we have, through Christ, towards God" (2 Cor 3:4).

It is indeed the problem of the supernatural psychology which here absorbs the attention of St. Paul. Why are Christians, fundamentally, so different from other people, so that their leaders can expect so much from them, can presume so much? No apostle, no priest of God could make to the people of God the appeals that are constantly being made if there were not, on their part, a responsiveness which is the ground of that confident action of their leaders. God has given His people a heart such as no other class of men possesses. It is the mystery of the Spirit, the pouring out of the Paraclete on the new people. In that Spirit and in nothing else the people of God possess their deep and far-reaching originality. Through that Spirit the whole supernatural order becomes congenital to the Christian; he is no longer a stranger, or a mere guest, but he has fellow-citizenship with the saints; he is of the family of God; he is, in a way, naturally supernatural, feeling perfectly at home in the religion of God.

Unless there were this intrinsic principle of spontaneous life coming from the depths in man where the Spirit of God has His abode, there would be no true people of God, there would be only a number of timid worshippers of God, who would never make His interests their own, who would never live and die with enthusiasm for God.

This doctrine of the new heart of the people of God, which is so evident in the inspired Scriptures, has been worked out theologically by the master of Catholic theology, St. Thomas Aquinas. In the First of the Second Part of the *Summa Theologica*, in which he lays down the fundamental principles of human behaviour, he establishes a comparison between the Old Law and the New. In his description of the New Law he accepts without hesitation the literalness of the prophetic utterances, corroborated as they are by the New Testament, and he declares, with great boldness I might say, that the New Law is nothing else than the grace of the Holy Spirit. Christians act, not directly through precepts and ordinances, but through the instincts of the Holy Ghost.

Unless we admit this immediateness of operation of the Holy Ghost as the guiding principle in the behavior of the new people, the much vaunted difference between the Old Law and the New Law would not exist. Christians are not only given higher and holier precepts, they are given the life-principle of conduct: the Holy Ghost. In this they differ from the old people of God. It is thus, and thus only that the great prophecies are accomplished. There can be no doubt as to the view taken by the great master of theology as to this matter. Unhesitatingly he draws the conclusions from the paeans of Jeremiah, of Ezekiel, of Paul of Tarsus, concerning the new order of things, when the Spirit Himself will be the Teacher.

We have, then, according to Aquinas, to believe in a universal spiritualization of the Christian People through the presence of the Holy Ghost. That spiritualization is the first thing, if not in time, at least in nature, and through it the Christian people accept everything else; from the greatest to the smallest we are vivified by the breath of the Spirit. The great Doctor is far from denying the existence and validity of precepts for the Christian; but he says that all those precepts are either a preparation for the coming of the Spirit who is the supreme Lawgiver, or they are practical results of the presence of that same Spirit. The Christian is either prepared for the Spirit by the full teaching of his faith or he acts in accordance with all the precepts of the law of love. But this preparation is not possible without the grace of the Spirit, nor is fidelity to all the teachings of the Gospel without the Spirit. So when everything has been said, the grace of the Spirit is the central element in the whole conduct of the people of God:

> The essential part (*principalitas*) of the New Law is the grace of the Holy Ghost, which is manifested in faith working through charity. And this grace men receive through the Son of God made Man, whose Humanity God filled with grace, which grace is being communicated to us.[2]

The Angelic Doctor answers many objections and in doing so he clarifies more and more the main idea of that divine instinct which is in the Christian people through the Holy Ghost as the principal source of their behavior. Thus he admits that even before Christ there were men who were thus endowed and acted spiritually; of them he says that they virtually belong to the New Law, in other words, to the new people of God. But the most serious objection will be the failures of Christians to act by that law of life: they sin and do the works of death.

No amount of human sinfulness, however, can interfere with the reality and greatness of the gift of the Spirit, though it is only in heaven that the New Law will sway men so powerfully as to render sin impossible, for in this life even a fervent believer can offend against God. Still the marvelous phenomenon which we call the heart of the people of God remains undiminished. It is quite certain that wherever Catholic faith dwells, there is in man a loyalty to God, an acceptance of the rights of God, a dread of the righteous judgements of God, which have all the character of profoundest sincerity.

It has been said sometimes that forced conversions of either Jews or heathens have resulted in generations of apparently normal Christians who still nurtured in their hearts a most distinct penchant for

---

2 *ST,* I q. 1, a. 58, ad 1

their old religion, with a dislike for the faith which had been forced upon them. If this be historically true we should have here an instance of what the people of God are not. Resentments of that nature are the very opposite of that alacrity of spirit in the faith which is in our phraseology the "heart of the people of God."

It will be objected, no doubt, that lukewarmness has been the evil of other Christians besides Saxon converts or Spanish Maranos; not all men, even during the best periods of the Christian people, have had hearts of flesh, breathed upon by the Holy Ghost. There have been hard-hearted Christians in immense numbers, as preachers and moralists of all times testify. This, of course, is a fact we need not explain away. But it does not by any means stultify the great prophecies, with their visions of a people entirely devoted to God; nor does it contradict the theological doctrine of the law of the Spirit. The mightiest river meets on its course rocks and boulders and even carries along with it stones, besides much other dead matter. The flow of the river is not impeded by this. So likewise the people of God have never ceased to worship God from the bottom of their hearts, in spite of many sinners in the midst of them.

St. Augustine, for one, has a delightful and playful passage in which he uses an older version of the Psalms, according to which the people of God is said to receive mercy "in the midst of the people." The people of God is a people full of fervor in the midst of men who also are, or ought to be, the people of God, but who are Without fervor:

> All those who receive the sacrament of Baptism of Christ are called Christians, but not all live worthily of that sacrament, for there are those concerning whom the Apostle says that they have the appearance of piety but deny its virtue. Nevertheless for the

sake of even that appearance of piety they are counted in the people of God, just as straw as well as grain is to be found on the threshing-floor whilst the process of threshing is going on. But will they be gathered one day into the barn? In the midst of the bad people of God is the good people of God.[3]

It is the everlasting question of "the people" of "the kingdom," of "the Church," possessing eternal life in its full sway and yet encountering obstacles within itself and scandals in its very midst at every turn. These foreign elements neither disunite the people, nor destroy the kingdom, nor desecrate the Church. The stream of life is the one unchallengeable reality.

Another quotation from St. Augustine's commentary on the same Psalm reveals the effort made by that great genius at solving this distressing and disturbing fact. In a truly delightful manner he teaches us how to see things in due proportion:

> Whosoever looks at a threshing-floor will be inclined to imagine that all that is there is nothing but straw. Bring along a man unversed in husbandry and he will think that it is labour lost to force oxen to trample on the straw and to get men to sweat under the heat of the burning sun in the effort to break the straw. But presently there will be visible a great heap ready to be sifted through the labor of the winnower. Then it will be made manifest what an abundance of wheat was hidden in all that heap of straw. (*Tunc procedet copia frumenti quae latebat in copia palearum*). You wanted to find the just, well then, you will find him![4]

---

3 St. Augustine, *Commentary on Psalm 47*
4 St. Augustine, *Commentary on Psalm 47*

✠ 5 ✠

THE SHEPHERD AND KING

CHRIST IN THE GOSPELS CAREFULLY AVOIDED SPEAKING of His followers, present and future, as of a people. We know the reason for this: to have declared Himself the founder of a new people, the leader of a new people, would have given to His enemies a ready opportunity for calumny. When the day of His enemies came they accused Him, before the Roman Governor, of stirring up the people and seducing them. In those days, as in our own, to head a popular movement was dangerous in the extreme; the national consciousness of the Jews was at white heat.

If Christ had declared Himself to be the head of a great people there could have been one meaning only to His words—He was putting Himself at the head of the nationalistic movement. This to the minds of the high priests would have produced merciless repression on the part of the Romans, so they could say with a fair amount of logic that if Jesus of Nazareth were allowed to win the people over to Himself the Romans would make an end of them and of their city:

The chief priests, therefore, and the Pharisees gathered a council and said: What do we, for this man doth many miracles? If we let him alone so, all will believe in him; and the Romans will come, and take away our place and nation (John 11:47-48).

Their reasoning is obvious: this wonder-worker can have only one end in view, to make himself the leader of the people. There will be an irrepressible national rallying round about him. The Romans, the overlords of Palestine will then have no choice, it must lead to the extermination of the Jewish race. The high priests and Pharisees were no lovers of Rome, but they were astute enough to see that their interests lay in the undisturbed continuance of that overlordship. For Christ, then, to call His own followers a "people" would have been surrendering that claim which He maintained to the very last, that He had not spoken anything which the whole World might not hear, anything that could compromise Him either with Caesar or with the Temple.

We have, however, in the sacred Gospels a glorious announcement of that same truth, but in a parable. It is Christ's emphatic declaration that He is a Shepherd, the good Shepherd, One who has many sheep, One who has a present flock and a future flock which He has to bring together, so that ultimately there will be only one flock and one Shepherd. Our Lord's divine words concerning Himself as the good Shepherd are the nearest approach we have from His lips to the description of a people.

To begin with, we ought to bear in mind that the metaphor of shepherd and flock did service for the concept of a ruler and his people over and over again in the inspired literature of the Scriptures and also in secular writings. Kings, in classical language, were spoken of as the shepherds of their subjects. Avoiding any terms that might have a political savor, Christ succeeded in making it clear to His contradictors that He would have the best and most faithful and most enthusiastic following any leader ever had. Moreover His following would be unassailable, superior to all hostile attacks:

> My sheep hear my voice. And I know them: and they follow me. And I give them life everlasting: and they shall not perish forever. And no man shall pluck them out of my hand. That which my Father hath given me is greater than all: and no one can snatch them out of the hand of my Father. I and the Father are one (John 10:27-30).

There can be no doubt as to the political meaning of these solemn utterances if we now take the word political in the sense of the leadership of human multitudes. Christ declares Himself to be such a leader and one that will never succumb, never disappoint His followers as had done so many who had risen in those days and led the people astray after themselves. In the last instance He appeals to His divinity, to His oneness with the Father, to explain the infallibility of His leadership. The Jews had asked Him point-blank the question whether He would be their leader:

> And it was the feast of the dedication at Jerusalem: and it was winter. And Jesus walked in the temple, in Solomon's porch. The Jews therefore came round about him and said to him: How long dost thou hold our souls in suspense? If thou be the Christ, tell us plainly (John 10:22-24).

On the lips of those men that query had only one meaning: "If thou be the promised leader of the people, tell us plainly and act accordingly."

Jesus does not want to be their leader; He answers them, "You do not believe because you are not of my sheep" (John 10:26). Yes, He is a leader, but not *their* leader; He has a following, but *they* are not that following; He has a people, but *they* are not His people.

Right through the Gospels we have the interplay of these two factors. Christ exhorts people to follow Him, which could only mean one thing, to be a true people surrounding Him: and Christ refuses to have a strictly political following, to be the hero of the nationalism of the times. These two factors are most prominent at an earlier period of His career when, after the multiplication of the bread, the people were on the point of taking Him by force and making Him king: "He fled again into the mountain, himself alone" (John 6:15). But this did not prevent Him from facing that multitude again on the day after in the synagogue of Caparnaum to declare to them that He was a leader indeed:

> All that the Father giveth to me shall come to me: and him that cometh to me, I will not cast out (John 6:37).

There also He gives utterance to the security possessed under His leadership by His following:

> Now this is the will of the Father who sent me: that of all He hath given me, I should lose nothing; but should raise it up again in the last day (John 6:39).

Christ, then, gives vent to His feelings about that heavenly leadership, a leadership consisting entirely of a supernatural attraction, of the Father's election, of His own life, of His Eucharist, of His flesh and of His blood; but such leadership is disappointing to the worldly mind; only a few could understand it:

> Then Jesus said to the twelve: Will you also go away? And Simon Peter answered him: Lord, to whom shall we go? Thou hast the words of eternal life (John 6:68-69).

But to return to the parable of the Shepherd. Christ enumerates all the characteristics of the supernatural nation: His people are flesh of His flesh and bone of His bone; such was the ancient and classical formula for expressing the relationship between the king and his people:

> Then all the tribes of Israel came to David in Hebron, saying: Behold we are thy bone and thy flesh (2 Sam 5:1).

Christ draws the picture of His own leadership by contrasts. The Jewish history of His days and those that preceded Him is full of disappointing leader ships, of efforts to be heard by the people, to be followed by them, to be acknowledged by them. Christ knew well the contemporary annals of His countrymen:

> All others, as many as have come, are thieves and robbers: and the sheep heard them not (John 10:8).

These would-be shepherds were after all strangers to the very men whose sympathies they tried to win:

> But a stranger they follow not, but fly from him, because they know not the voice of strangers (John 10:5).

Then again, none of them had a living interest in his following; they were hirelings, the sheep were not their own and in the days of danger they fled and left the flock to the wolf.

What is so adorable in this comparison that Christ makes between Himself and the shepherd is the assertion that between Himself and

His own, His people, His sheep, there is a relationship which is akin to blood relationship. In the heart of the shepherd there is the voice of the blood, and likewise in the hearts of the sheep there is the voice of blood; blood answering blood. Whatever may have been the transient authority of party leaders over their followers, such authority did not stand the test of time, the test of peril. In the case of Christ, on the contrary, the first act is this, to give His life for the sheep: moreover to them He gives life and gives it ever more abundantly; no human leadership can do this, even were it disinterested, which as a rule it is not. Christ could truly have said nothing stronger in order to convey the truth that He meant to be the leader of an immense people:

> And when he hath let out his own sheep, he goeth before them: and the sheep follow him, because they know his voice (John 10:4).

Between Himself and His people there is an understanding which is their exclusive privilege:

> I am the good shepherd, and I know mine, and mine know me. As the Father knoweth me, and I know the Father (John 10:14-15).

If such words were used by a human leader concerning his following we should, of course, pronounce him to be a madman because it is not in the power of man thus to command and thus to be obeyed; but with Christ such claims seem natural. We know that what He said in the Gospel has been realized in history: there has been this pressing of millions of souls round the divine Shepherd; there has been this mutual understanding; Christ's life is in man and Christ's death and resurrection are the ultimate appeals to human loyalty.

Truly there could be no clearer definition of the character of the people of God than the sayings of our Lord concerning Himself as the Good Shepherd. The whole mystery of the Incarnation is pressed into service in order to explain the constitutional principles of that new people, the flock of Christ. Christ, by the very characteristics of His personality, is supremely fitted to be the leader of a people. He is truly the born ruler because in all things He is ultimate reality; His power is the power of God; His vigilance is the providence of God; His love is love unto death, and the pasture on which He feeds His sheep is nothing else than His own life. His people are truly His flesh and His bone because they are born from His very substance.

Let us once more emphasize the contrast. So many men there were striving after the mastery over men, but that mastery they could not attain without killing, without scattering; murder was the guilt of every leader who had even temporary success. Opposed to that leadership stands Christ's mastery over man, Where there is only one death—His own, and Where everything else is life:

> This proverb Jesus spoke to them. But they understood not What he spoke to them (John 10:6).

Nothing prepared those poor men for the idea of a leadership whose sole power and efficacy would be in the intangible realities of the spiritual world.

✠ 6 ✠

The Rights of the People of God

IT ALWAYS HAS BEEN AND IT ALWAYS WILL BE A DIFFICULTY for many to accept the fact that there is a people of God. Why should there be this privilege, this differentiation, between men and men on the part of Him who is the Creator and the Judge of all?

The difficulty in admitting this state of exception is peculiar, not to those who are outside the exception but to those who are inside it, to those who are the beneficiaries of it. The man who does not belong to the people of God starts with the assumption that there is no such people: that is the very essence of heathenism. So he will not bother his head about the theological question how God, out of the mass of humanity, constitutes His people. It is the son of the kingdom who will be overcome at times by an impression of dread lest, by calling himself a member of a privileged race, he should commit the sin of presumption. It is only those who have faith in God's power of election who will be puzzled by the mystery of that election: why God elects and selects at all, instead of dealing with all men alike.

Yet it is the very first quality of the people of God to know their status, to recognize their privilege, to say that not to all men has God done as He has done unto them. The great reproach of God against the prototype of the people of God, His ancient people, the Jewish nation, was this: that they made light at times of their unique position, that they were content to be no more than the races which surrounded them. God expected them to consider themselves as a peculiar people, endowed with qualities no other people on earth possessed; He never rebuked them for pride in their election, but He did rebuke them severely for forgetfulness of that election. The new and veritable people of God are expected to make profession unceasingly of their exclusive position in the designs of God's providence. Any slackness in the realization of their privilege is a great spiritual disaster; it is a victory of the enemy of the people of God.

In order to understand the workings of this divine nationalism let us expound more amply the remarks just made that only the people of God are capable of being aware that there is such a people and that therefore they alone can know the rights and the claims of that people. The infidel world not only practically but also theoretically rejects *ex toto* any such possibility. This is a feature of infidelity to which perhaps we pay but little attention, but it is very evident. Infidelity takes it for granted that all men are equal, that they are equally low, equally degraded; materialism, which is another word for infidelity, by the very nature of its tenets excludes all higher calling, every kind of selection that is not natural selection. It is not against the spirit of materialism to accept selection and election in the biological sense, but it is entirely contrary to its spirit to let any category of men be raised above the laws of universal humanity.

The Christian then may rest assured that when he claims the right for the people of God to exist as a separate entity he is doing a thing that concerns himself exclusively. He has in himself the justification of such behavior, the motives of such an attitude; the pagan world cannot help him there, it simply remains unbelieving with regard to a matter that to a Christian is vital; we know ourselves to be the people of God through divine revelation, through the assurance of the Spirit of God; we do the works of God, but outside revelation our claim has no foundation. Accordingly, in laying down what we might call the constitutional principles of the people of God we ask no man's leave, we beg no man's favor, we appeal to no man's patronage; the people of God have in themselves the justification of all their claims and pretensions.

Our first and unalienable claim is, of course, that the people of God are a sovereign people, that their activities as people of God are under no other control than that of God Himself. All that can be said of the sovereignty of a human State must be predicated of that super human State, the people of God, and, of course, in much ampler form. No interference can be brooked, the limits of that sovereignty are as sharply outlined as the political boundaries of any nation on earth; no Christian need hesitate for a moment in his belief in the sovereignty of the people to which he is spiritually attached.

With this sense of sovereignty there co-exists in the Christian mind the knowledge how to deal with all things, above all, how to treat with powers that are not spiritually supreme but are institutions of a lower order. Now it is distinctively the gift of the people of God to reconcile diversities of jurisdiction. A whole book could be written, not only on the theory of the double allegiance but on its practice, as it has been carried out for centuries. It may be laid down as an incontrovertible truth that the people of God have always been in the right in their contacts with secular powers, that is to say, they have never refused the secular power the measure of acknowledgement and obedience due to it. It would almost seem to be the first and most immediate result of that sense of spiritual sovereignty to have what we might truly call the right political appreciation, in dealing with other sovereignties of a lower order. At the very first hour, when in the power of the Spirit the liberty of the people of God was proclaimed, behavior towards the secular sovereignties was learned as it were naturally and applied most consistently:

> Let every soul be subject to higher powers. For there is no power but from God: and those that are are ordained of God (Rom 13:1).

From this line of conduct the people of God have never deflected. That gift of discrimination seems to be one of the first supernatural endowments no doubt an aspect of the gift of counsel which the sevenfold Spirit bestows on the Church. For this reason one need never be surprised at that obtuseness of the non-Catholic with regard to what we ought to call the double allegiance of the Catholic; allegiance to the sovereign people of God and allegiance to the earthly nation to which he belongs. Not a man in a thousand among non-Catholics can understand the practical possibility of this double loyalty which to us Catholics is an obvious fact, the easiest thing in the world. This makes one believe in the completely supernatural character of the gift of discrimination which is the counterpart of our faith in the sovereignty of the people of God.

The liturgical expression of Catholic sentiment leaves no doubt as to the place which the people of God ought to hold:

THE RIGHTS OF THE PEOPLE OF GOD 49

O Lord, save thy people and bless thine inheritance: Govern them and exalt them forever. Day by day we bless thee and we praise thy name forever.

Elsewhere the Church prays thus:

O God, who in all the children of thy Church hast manifested by the voice of the holy prophets in every place of thy dominion that thou art the sower of good seed and the cultivator of chosen branches, grant to thy people, who are called by thee by the names of vineyards and corn, that the unsightliness of thorns and briars being removed, they may produce Worthy and abundant fruit.[5]

Whenever the people of God is prayed for there is no sort of hesitancy, no kind of timidity in the demand; the people is entitled to all the blessings in heaven and on earth which God has destined for mankind. The people is exhorted to pray for its own exaltation through God's mercy and for the downfall of His enemies. It can ask boldly for temporal prosperity because to that a people is entitled; but it also asks for strength in adversity because it feels itself to be a sinful people. One thing alone is completely absent from the liturgical texts in which there is mention of the people of God, I mean doubt and hesitation concerning the rights and claims of that people:

Almighty and everlasting God, who dost govern all things both in heaven and earth; mercifully hear the prayers of thy people and grant us thy peace in our days.[6]

---

5 Prayer on Holy Saturday
6 Collect for Second Sunday after Epiphany

✠ 7 ✠

The King and Reaper

IF A NUMBER OF MEN WERE TO BELIEVE IN THE MYSTERY of the Incarnation, this community of faith would not necessarily constitute those believers into a people; it is necessary for them to look upon the Incarnate God as their common leader, their universally accepted chief in order to deserve the appellation of the people of God. The kingship of Christ is no accidental embellishment of the fundamental dogma of the Incarnation, it is, on the contrary, an essential constituent of that dogma. From the very beginning the mystery of the Son of God is a mystery of active kingship:

> He shall be great and shall be called the Son of the Most High. And the Lord God shall give unto him the throne of David his father: and he shall reign in the house of Jacob forever. And of his kingdom there shall be no end (Luke 1: 32-33).

Even in St. John's Gospel, where there seems to be a preponderance of the life-giving mission of the Word made Flesh, there soon transpires that other mission—the kingship:

> Nathanael answered him and said: Rabbi: thou art the Son of God. Thou art the King of Israel. Jesus answered and said to him: Because I said unto thee, I saw thee under the fig tree, thou believest: greater things than these shalt thou see. And he saith to him: Amen, amen, I say to you, you shall see the heavens opened, and the angels of God ascending and descending upon the Son of man (John 1:49-51).

There can be no doubt as to the spontaneous and persistent response of true Christian believers of all times to this hidden claim of the Incarnate Word, His kingship. The Christian people have always believed themselves to be directly under the leadership of a heavenly monarch, not only in their individual life but as a nation of sanctified men and women. It would be the easiest thing in the world to adduce endless testimony to that faith, say, from the year 800 to the year 1600; the Christian nations in most practical ways professed the kingship of Christ; the Son of God in the glory of the Father was looked upon by every Christian as the ruler of the Catholic society.

But we have abundant witness of a yet earlier period through which it is made clear that the kingship of Christ was an accepted fact amongst all Catholics at all times. Christ had overthrown paganism and established Himself as the sovereign of the world that had been converted. Schisms and heresies necessarily meant a diminution in the fervor of that faith, because everyone who separated himself from the Christian society became, unavoidably, an exile from the kingdom of Christ, a stranger, nay, even an outcast. The greater the fervor of the Christian people, and the more vivid their faith, the more intense was their loyalty to the supreme king. The Christian could not in the past, and cannot today, look upon the Incarnate Word of God in love only; he sees in Him the mightiest of all powers, whose claims are superior to all others and who has every right to ask for unhesitating loyalty.

There has always been in the Christian faith in Christ's kingship a quality which we might call the quality of longanimity; not only have Christians understood that the ruling of the Son of God is a mysterious activity, full of reverence for man's freedom, but they have been patient in a positive fashion with the delays of the divine judgements; they know that their King is exerting the fullness of His powers even when iniquity, for the time being, seems to be triumphant.

here is nothing narrow-minded, there is nothing fanatical in the following of the leadership of the Word Incarnate; external triumphs and successes of a temporal nature are not indispensable to the Catholic faith in the kingship of Christ. That leadership is above all things a leadership of souls, bringing souls from darkness into light, from the power of Satan to God. It is, translated into human terms, the great battle that took place in heaven between the spirits themselves. The battle of Christ here on earth has the characteristics of that heavenly conflict, of that contest between two opposing armies of spirits. It is therefore to be taken for granted that the incidents of Christ's kingship are the features proper to a war of spirits. No Christian is surprised at any time at the magnitude and the vehemence of the hostility manifested by men against Christ; it is truly the conflict with the powers in heavenly places:

> For our wrestling is not against flesh and blood; but against principalities and powers, against the rulers of the world of this darkness, against the spirits of wickedness in the high places (Eph 6:12).

Great material losses may be demanded of the people of God by the very nature of that conflict. Riches, power, influence, honor, taken in their more material sense, may at times be a heavy burden for the Christian warriors; they will be asked, mercilessly, without remorse, to shed them, so as to be rendered fit for the wrestling. Such strippings should not and do not weaken the faith of the Christian people in their king; nay, even desertions do not frighten them because it may be necessary for the final victory that there be a division of spirits, as it was in heaven when there was the great war between Michael and Lucifer.

All these things, as we said, are understood by the people of God, and their loyalty to Christ resembles the loyalty of a people to their ancient and well-proved dynasty, not like transient enthusiasms for the successful upstart of the present hour. The Christian people feel instinctively that their king is unconquerable because He has been victorious for so long. They are not in need of signs and wonders, though such flamboyant testimonies of power may be necessary to the false Christs, to the false leaders.

The most manifest sign of the presence of that great king in the midst of the affairs of this world is this very thing—that at no time has it been possible since His coming for men to settle down in peace to a merely natural policy of life. Unceasingly they are being troubled, we might almost say by the specter of Christ. Their very efforts to suppress Christ give away their true sentiments: they are frightened of Him and of His power. They feel Him to be an irresistible intruder into human affairs; they must, first of all, be free of Him before they can dream of establishing men's lives on an exclusively human basis.

This terror inspired by Christ in His enemies is to the Christian people the second evidence of the reality of His kingship; the first evidence, of course, being their own loving faith in that sovereignty. For up to now humanity's case has never been like this, that on the one hand there is the group of Christians, more or less numerous, passionately devoted to a heavenly king, whilst on the other hand there is the world living in absolute indifference towards that king, or even in Complete ignorance of Him. There is neither indifference nor ignorance: there is hatred, resentment, terror. Christ is a divine power of disturbance; Christ's kingship is an ominous menace to the city of evil and as a menace He is known to that city. It is always feared that His claims and His rights may be enforced again. The terror of His Name is one of the most palpable realities in the history of the last two thousand years, and in the eyes of the Christian people that fear is nothing else than the actual manifestation of the heavenly supremacy of the Son of God.

Periodically nations set out to prepare for the time when the Name of Christ will be extinguished, will be an unknown quantity. "In two or three generations," they say, "men will forget all about Christ; we shall take care of the young in such wise that no one will remember the Name of Jesus in less than half a century."

We may just grant to them that they might be successful in turning away a whole generation from the love of Christ; but indifference to Christ, ignorance of Christ, will be a state of society hopelessly unattainable. A nation of fanatical haters of Christ may come out of the machinations of the sons of Belial, but not a period of blissful oblivion of the great Name. It will always be true that ' he who not for Christ is against Him in direct and positive fashion. Such a spiritual outlook, positive love and positive hatred, is the very essence of kingship, for kingship with the Son of God is more than life and love, it is a potent impact on the freewill of man.

So we read of Christ's kingship in astonishing terms. It is always a "breaking" in the day of His anger. He will "break" the kings, He will "break" them as the potter's vessel is broken; He will "break" the world lest it settle down to a comfortable oblivion of Himself:

> The Lord hath said to me: Thou art my son; this day have I begotten thee. Ask of me, and I will give thee the Gentiles for thy inheritance and the utmost parts of the earth for thy possession. Thou shalt rule them with a rod of iron and shalt break them in pieces like a potter's vessel (Ps 2:7-9).

As already insinuated, nothing but a completely orthodox Christology can keep alive in the Christian people a living appreciation of Christ's kingship. There are in the history of mankind, and even in the history of the Church, dark spaces of such dimensions that no light except it be infinite could reach their end; it is only the Sun of Justice, Christ, the All-holy, that sends rays beyond the dark ranges.

The faith of the Christian people in Christ's king ship has precisely this character—it looks upon the presence of the sun in the firmament before looking on the earth's surface; the sun in his power is the symbol of kingship; in other words, the Christian people have an instinctive insight into the personal greatness of the Son of God; His incommensurable sanctity is more than an accepted fact, it is a religious sentiment. From the height of that sanctity they contemplate the attitudes of men and they know that no multitudes, however numerous, could through their blasphemies and their denials stop the victorious course of the divine Sun of Justice.

Besides possessing longanimity, the Christian faith in Christ's kingship contains also far sightedness; it has the gift of appreciating the value of lengthy preparations, it knows that years and even centuries of human events are not final providences but are mere preparations for some mighty manifestation of grace which will be shown forth in its day by the Lord of Glory:

> I charge thee before God who quickeneth all things, and before Christ Jesus who gave testimony under Pontius Pilate, a good confession: That thou keep the commandment without spot, blameless, unto the coming of our Lord Jesus Christ, which in his times he shall show, who is the Blessed and only Mighty, the King of kings and Lord of lords. Who only hath immortality and inhabiteth light inaccessible: whom no man hath seen, nor can see: to whom be honor and empire everlasting. Amen (Tim 6:13-16).

It is in connection with Christ's kingship that the words of the Lord became poignantly true: "Blessed is he that shall not be scandalized in me" (Matt 11:6). The people of God have never been scandalized by Christ's dealings with the world. They have understood that their mighty sovereign came, not to destroy but to save souls, that His empire is above all a power of mercy and that, even in the days of His anger He remembers leniency.

The Apocalypse of St. John may be truly called the inspired account of Christ's royalty. It is, as we all know, a terrible series of tableaux showing Christ in His role of a combatant king fighting the dragon, the Beast, and the false prophet. It is also extremely realistic in its presentment of the fortunes of the people of God. Of the Beast, the enemy of Christ, it is said that "it was given unto him to make war with the saints and to overcome them" (Rev 13:7). But this is only an incident; the words that follow give us the real issues:

> He that shall lead into captivity shall go into captivity: he that shall kill by the sword must be killed by the sword. Here is the patience and the faith of the saints (Rev 13:10).

The patience and the faith of the saints will have the last word. The victory of the Beast over the saints in temporal matters is preparing the downfall of that hostile force; it is given as an absolute axiom that he that shall kill by the sword must be killed by the sword. The political upheavals of this world, with their massacres, are the execution of Christ's judgements.

In spite of itself, then, the world works for the final consummation of the counsels of the supreme king; so we have that other inspired presentment of the Son of God in glory when He is made to appear on a white cloud not only as a crowned king but as a reaper with a sharp sickle. He is one that has Waited for the ripeness of the harvest and when things have reached maturity through the processes of an infinitely patient providence, then, like a flash of lightning, the sharp sickle is thrust into the wheat of human existences:

> And I saw: and behold a white cloud and upon the cloud one sitting like to the Son of Man, having on his head a crown of gold and in his hand a sharp sickle. And another angel came out from the temple, crying with a loud voice to him that sat upon the cloud: Thrust in thy sickle and reap, because the hour is come to reap. For the harvest of the earth is ripe. And he that sat on the cloud thrust his sickle into the earth: and the earth was reaped (Rev 14:14-16).

This combination of kingship and reaping is indeed the most satisfying presentment of the mystery of Christ's royalty; great as the king is and vast as His power He awaits the hour of ripeness, He even awaits the call of the creature, the angel that reminds Him of the whiteness of the harvest, before He thrusts in the sickle; but with a mighty arm, with irresistible vigor He reaps the harvest of the earth in a moment when the hour has struck. Thus the people of God love to look upon their king with a crown on His head, sitting on the white clouds of heaven and abiding patiently His time for victorious action.

In the sacred Gospels our Lord had already described the slow and hidden process of ripening to be followed, almost suddenly, by the act of reaping, as being the distinctive mark of the kingdom of God:

> And he said: So is the kingdom of God, as if a man should cast seed into the earth, and should sleep and rise, night and day, and the seed should spring and grow up whilst he knoweth not. For the earth of itself bringeth forth fruit, first the blade, then the ear, afterwards the full corn in the ear. And when the fruit is brought forth, immediately he putteth in the sickle, because the harvest is come (Mark 4:26-29).

This maturity of the divine seed is brought about through the double influence of earthly events and heavenly vitalities, "For the earth of itself bringeth forth" (Mark 4:28). Human history, with all its vicissitudes, is a slow maturing of the plans of God, but the seed itself, the faith in Christ, is of heavenly origin and has the power of counteracting evil to an infinite degree. We may make the words of St. Paul the universal motto of Christ's rulings:

> To them that love God all things work together unto good: to such as, according to his purpose, are called to be saints (Rom 8:28).

It will indeed be one of the joys of the elect for all eternity to contemplate in the light of God the true meaning of all the human events that prepare the elect for their great glory; it will be manifested then how, when man thought only of evil, he was really the artisan of God's judgments.

✠ 8 ✠

THE ACTIVITIES OF THE PEOPLE OF GOD

It is my opinion that we shall never do justice to historic Christianity unless we supplement the notion of "Church" with that of "people." I do not, of course, say that radically these two terms do not signify the same reality, but as our minds are bound to separate, to give preference, now to one aspect, now to another, we shall be much more fair to Catholicism if we allow Catholics to be the 'people ' beside being the "Church" of God. The concept of a Church is, from necessity, mystical and sacramental. Now not all things are seen in due proportion if they are looked at from the mystical and sacramental angle, and there is much in the history of Christianity which is narrated most fairly if it is said that a people, the people of God, has been at work.

Our present-day spiritual condition, again, is understood more completely if we understand ourselves to be the people of God besides knowing ourselves to be the Church. In other words, to whichever term we give the preference, the Christian Church is a society that is also a people in quite the technical sense of the word; and again the Christian people is a nation that is essentially a Church. This double mode of union amongst several is indeed exclusive to Catholicism. It may be said that the whole adverse tendency from the sixteenth century onwards has been this: first, to discriminate between "people" and "Church," so that it be no longer allowed that there is a people of God though there be still a Church of God; and then to discriminate between Church and religion, so that a man could still call himself a religious man though he be an enemy of the Church. A so-called effort at purifying the Church has led many to separate the Church from mankind, to isolate her, to make her almost invisible and superhuman.

Now a people is never universally refined; it is a crowd. It would seem at times as if we did not want the Bride of Christ to be in the midst of a turbulent people. It is, of course, possible to express all the activities of Catholicism in ecclesiastical terms, so that everything the millions of Catholics ever did they did as a Church, for the Church, and all their labors are Church functions. But it will easily be perceived that if we consider the Catholic multitudes as the people of God, their activities will be more readily explicable, they will find their proper place and level.

To take a famous instance: We may, of course, read the crusades in the light of our theology *de Ecclesia* ("of the Church"—the Church concept does cover these great wars of religion), but if we start from the assumption that there was in Europe in the eleventh century a true people of God, who behaved like a people, crusades fall into line much more readily. A people of God will fight for the tomb of their God. If, on the other hand, we give to the Church concept an exclusively mystical significance we shall have nothing but condemnation for those generous efforts of our valiant forefathers. We might say that to remain in their villages and make their prayers in their own Churches would have been the more congenital task of the devout Catholic.

Such instances we may multiply. But I feel certain that anyone who approaches the history of the Catholic Church as the history of the people of God will have a better understanding of the past as well as of the present. Perhaps the very title "history of the Church" has a narrowing effect and creates a prejudice from the start, as the historian expects everything to be weighed in the ecclesiastical scales.

I should be the very last man to restrict the amplitude of the definition of the Church: all the narrowing down has been done by men who were not loyal to the Church. But at no time is the Church so clearly seen in the fullness of her mission as when she is defined as the people of God, dwelling on this earth. All those elements of life, all those activities that are necessary to the prosperity of a people thus become integral portions of Church life.

We may put it in this fashion: say that there is a very strong, a very powerful, a very prolific nation, of a hundred million souls, a political unit, taking now the terms "nation" and "political" in their natural and obvious meaning. Let us suppose that the gift of the faith were, for the time being, restricted to that nation, all other inhabitants of the earth being then either hostile or indifferent to the faith (it is not impossible for Catholicism, at least, for a period to be thus limited geographically); the point I want to illustrate is that this great nation, being universally Catholic and believing, would be *ipso facto* and very ostensibly the people of God on this earth.

Now there is no activity in that people which would not be directly the work of the people of God; all their exertions, all their enterprises, all their labors of whatever kind, would have this end, the life of that people of God. Industry, art, letters, science, government, peace and war, everything would be imbued with the spirit of service unto God; the laborer in the field, the craftsman in his shop, the artist in his studio, the lecturer in the university, the young in the playing fields, the soldier in the camp—they would all be the supports of the people of God. There is no kind of activity that would be amiss, that would be outside the framework of the supernatural nationhood. Such a people would put its principal resources into divine worship, into the acts of religion; it would glorify God in every possible way, there would be no end to its enterprises in order to magnify the Name of Christ.

Such a tableau is not a mere dream, it is What Catholicism aims at. Any diminution is bewailed by the friends of God as a step towards apostasy. The realization of this ideal is simply the Catholic plan fully carried out, it is the Church in her entirety; but, as I have said repeatedly, it is more directly the description of the people of God than of the mystical Body of Christ, anyhow according to certain modern ways of conceiving that mystical Body. The ruling powers of the nation we have sketched would, of necessity, be the rulers of the people of God, obedient to the dictates of the Catholic faith, obedient to the spiritual rule of that faith. There can be no doubt that Catholicism aims at such a state of things.

Catholicism would like to see the whole human race endowed with the qualities which I have attributed to that hypothetical nation in the first chapter of this book. Catholicism says that mankind, as mankind, ought to be the people of God. Indeed the human race would have been the people of God if it had not fallen in Adam. But the Fall has not altered God's plans: God expects the race to serve Him completely and we may say that the original idea which the

Creator had in putting man on this earth has never been deflected from its first purpose. The corruption of men and their idolatry made God choose His own people in the Old Testament in preparation for the new people, the Christian world, who are today the manifestation of God's first plan to people this earth with His own subjects, to have on this planet His own nation.

It is against the best Catholic tradition to watch with indifference the secularization of the human race, in the comfortable persuasion that the Church has her own exclusive life. The Church must be human even when she is restricted in numbers, and although much can be said in order to bring out the Church's superiority to worldly advantages, we can never detach the Church from human activity.

Believers, wherever they are, must show their faith in external works, in deeds that prove that they consider themselves a people who serve God. It is certain that for a very long time Catholicism considered itself in the light of the people of God. The picture we have drawn is not as much a figment of the imagination as might appear; most of it was a reality in the middle ages, and if we want to give in a phrase the difference between our own times and the early centuries, we need only say that during those periods of faith men were profoundly convinced that they were the people of God, a conviction much less alive in our days.

There certainly could be nothing more diametrically opposed to the aspirations of Catholicism than to allocate to the notion of "people" an exclusively temporal and secular meaning, so that Catholicism would have nothing left except the internal grace; deprive Catholicism of the power of external manifestation is to make it impossible for the people of God to exist. The Catholic Church even in the days of her greatest unpopularity was always a people, though a people that was humbled and broken down. It seems to have been reserved to our own days to make the attempt to drive Catholicism so much back on itself that it dare not call itself a people any more. This is, of course, anti-Christ. It was as we know attempted at least in a haphazard way by Julian the Apostate, whose policy it was to isolate Christians from every contact with corporate civilization.

How this plan is being renewed in our days needs no elaboration; everything seems to conspire at the present stage of human development to make the existence of a people of God an impossibility; this however no Catholic will accept. We may be a people living under duress but we are a people; duress is not against nationhood, but as history has proved again and again it is its very foster-mother. Was not Egyptian slavedom the cradle of the first people of God?

It would not be superfluous for us Catholics to apply to our supernatural nationhood the lessons which we have learned so well from the racial struggles of many a European people of today. We have accepted it as axiomatic that no outside force can destroy a people; thus we argue also that no temporal adversity can destroy the people of God. We admit the ups and downs in the course of that people's history to an unpredictable extent; we do not expect uninterrupted periods of all-round prosperity. In fact, inequalities of condition of every kind seem to be the more normal state, inequalities not only in fortune but in the distribution of God's gifts.

One of the great advantages that come from looking habitually upon the multitude of the friends of God as upon a people is precisely this facility of reconciling our mind with the inequalities which are seen everywhere amongst those who work for God. A people is built up of inequalities. To make of equality a nation's ideal is, of course, an illusion, as history proves so well.

The people of God would be the very last people to be the victims of such an error; they are essentially a multitude composed of the big and the small. There is endless variety in their endowments, in their powers, in their offices, in their graces, in their lives. They have one thing in common: they all go to God. But then the God to whom they go is not an indivisible point; He is, on the contrary, by definition an immensity. Not only diversity, but inequality to an astonishing degree is to be found in the people of God. Diversity we could easily admit; God being infinitely rich can give to His creatures an inexhaustible variety of gifts, so that each one may glory in his possessions; we might speak of them as equally rich though differently so.

But the people of God are endowed, not only with variety but also with inequality; there are those who are granted more and those who are given less, and those differences of measure are willed by God. He loves to have a people composed of giants and dwarfs, we might say, of the strong and of the feeble, of the quick and of the slow; He is not angry with the little ones for being little because He is the One who made the great and the small alike. Nor is this inequality merely a transient arrangement: His people will be so forever and ever, even in the glories of eternity.

There is nothing in Catholic theology on nature and grace that compels us to believe that it is God's intention for all men to strive after equal heights; on the contrary, at every turn in his survey of the activities of divine grace and human co-operation, the Catholic divine is brought up against these realities of astonishing inequalities. To admit the existence of them is not only the solution of many puzzles and scandals, but it is the source of a positive intellectual contentment. It is truly beautiful to see the mighty Lord of heaven and earth caressing with the hand of His power the nascent good-will of the semi-developed human individual, and to find Him at the same time holding the hand of the athlete in the arena of spiritual exertion.

Inequality, then, is everywhere in the people of God. There are the historic inequalities which affect the various generations of the followers of God so profoundly. Human history, as everyone knows, is a long succession of inequalities of condition. To rectify those inequalities was never in the power of any generation of men; they were born into them and accepted them as their natural life. Their degree of knowledge, their mode of civilization, their powers over nature made a setting entirely conformable to their needs and their desires. In that setting they worked out their destiny and God did not ask more of them. From the earliest times there was at work the providence of the talents which Christ in His day was to express in a magnificent parable. Man was pleasing to God, not when he did more than his measure, but when he traded with his talents, were they one, were they ten. Trading with one talent never made him the equal of another who traded with ten, but it made him a faithful servant, a friend of God, one whose activity was complete and who deserved an unqualified encomium.

When we consider the varieties of circumstances under which men have had to live we may sometimes ask ourselves whether their chances were big enough to do any good whatever. Let us not throw the blame on God, let us not accuse Him of having been less generous to any generation of men. In the words of St. Paul, "never did He leave Himself without testimony" (Acts 14:17), and the men of the most dismal periods of history, as we might call certain epochs, were the people of God in the full meaning of the term, and God was pleased with them.

There is nothing so contrary to the very constitution of the people of God as any unwillingness to accept the inequalities of condition with generosity. Those inequalities, in the inspired canticles of the people of God, are not matters of regret but occasions of divine praise; God is glorified because He is the God of the great and the small, because with Him there dwells the lofty spirit and the humble child of man. To set out to destroy inequality is to make a frontal attack on a divine dispensation, a prevarication which is sure to be visited with utmost severity on the part of the Creator; the more man tries to level inequality, the greater will be the gaps between man and man.

This love of the divine inequalities gives to God's people a great patience with the weaknesses and infirmities of the brethren. Christians have no difficulty in believing literally that God has made the poor, that God gives sickness, that, according to the Gospel narrative, a man may be born blind not because he or his parents had sinned, but unto the glory of God, that God might be glorified in him. It is not the will of God that man should be perfect at all times; it is the will of God rather, that through a long process he should reach, not all perfection, but that perfection which is destined for him individually; nor is he always meant to reach that point on this earth. God will bring him to perfection in His own way and in His own hour.

✠ 9 ✠

God's Patience with His People

Many a sermon has been preached from Christian pulpits on the patience of God towards man. The more often we speak of that divine attribute, patience, the greater will be our service to the cause of religion. No doubt it requires a faith that is sure of itself to make of the patience of God one of its commonplaces; for at first sight it would seem that nothing could do less to further the interests of religion than belief in God's patience.

Such a confidence, the detractor would say, must, of necessity, breed spiritual indolence; man will bank on God's patience with him and in the meantime offend in every possible way in the conviction that God's patience is inexhaustible. The dogma of the divine patience is indeed essentially Christian: a human-made religion could not afford a Godhead that has patience with the iniquities of men because the moral order would be endangered by the supposition of a divinity that could not wax angry at the sight of iniquity.

The way in which faith in God's patience has become part of the Christian ethical system is very interesting indeed; God's patience is not, according to St. Paul, a mere negative thing, a sort of divine indifference; it is, on the contrary, like all other divine attributes, a most active force, a disposition of divine providence to give time to men for repentance:

> Despisest thou the riches of his goodness and patience and long-suffering? Knowest thou not that the benignity of God leadeth thee to penance (Rom 2:4)?

The longanimity of God is the patience of the worker, not the repose of the idler. In human experience all great achievements are the fruit of an endless period of unceasing activity: God's patience is this very thing, the perseverance of the strong will. Thus God may be spoken of as a patient worker, untiringly busy to prepare, to create, and to crown the work of salvation. Therefore in Christian spirituality there is no making light of the treasures of God's patience because there is the knowledge that divine forbearance is not an overlooking of the evil deeds, but a further chance for doing penance.

In practice we find that none of those who are enamored at of the divine attribute of patience in their own case would abuse it. They wonder at God's longanimity with the sinner in general. Nor does the confirmed sinner find comfort in the thought of God's patience, as his state of habitual estrangement from God renders him indifferent to God's judgement of his life. Of him St. Paul says:

> What if God, willing to show his wrath and to make his power known, endured with much patience vessels of wrath, fitted for destruction (Rom 9:22)?

God's patience with His own people may be called proverbial: it is one of the commonplaces of the Scriptures. God is represented as carrying the burdens of His ancient people till He drops them from sheer disgust and even then He does not reject them forever. There is every reason to claim for the new people of God, the Christian people, that same advantage; with infinite patience God deals with His people, with His elect, with those in whom there is the seal of Christ. One might say that God has promised and guaranteed infinite patience on His part through the whole economy of Christianity. He has placed, right in the center of Christianity, the rainbow of patience, the covenant that He will never destroy His people because He has given them the infallible means of constantly appeasing His anger through the power of the Blood of the Lamb.

To read the history of the Christian people in forgetfulness of that divine mystery of forbearance would be a very narrow naturalism. God's patience with the Christian people is a covenanted dispensation, it is an outcome of the Redemption, it is a portion of the Incarnation, of that mystery which makes indissoluble the union of human nature with Divinity in the Person of Jesus Christ. After that covenant God can no more reject His people than He can reject His Son. God's patience is His resolve not to allow the gates of hell to prevail against the Church; now such a resolve is a creative act, like the promise made in the days of Noah that the seasons will succeed each other without confusion for all time. The people in their multitudes will be treated by God with infinite considerateness for the love of His Son; He will forgive their sins, He will not allow their aberrations to have their full consequences, He will make mercy prevail over justice, He will do infinitely more than would be strictly necessary to maintain in existence the Church He has founded.

The patience of God has, of course, for its object the sins of the people; God bears with our infirmities, God puts His hand under our head in our very falls; the Christian people have every right to appropriate to themselves all those magnificent scriptural expressions. If Peter is ordered to forgive his brother till seventy times seven a hint is given to him as to the spirit of the New Law. The only return God expects for His forbearance is this: that the Christian also should bear with his brother.

It is evident that this faith in God's patience with His people creates a temperament in the Catholic mind, in the Catholic judgement of ecclesiastical events. To expect the course of Church history to be such that there is no call for God's patience is truly absurd from the Christian point of view. All we know of God's intentions through the Incarnation makes it clear that from the very start God has put at the disposal of His Church an inexhaustible treasure of patience on His part; it is the Church's supernatural capital, on it the people of God can safely bank. There is no sin so big, there is no disorder so prolonged as to exhaust God's patience with us. We ought never in our zeal for sanctity to dream of an order of things in which there would no longer be room for the longanimity of God; God has not promised any such order of things, but He has made a definite pact with His Son that He will forgive His people all their sins.

One seems to hear the jibe of the rationalist who says that a religion which counts thus boldly on God's patience could hardly lay claim to heroicity. Be it said here that the heroicity of Christian sanctity is not human effort in its highest degree; it is at all times intimately associated with the exercise of humility, that humility which makes a man say *Misericordias Domini in aeternum cantabo* ("I will sing the mercies of God forever"). More than anyone else the Christian saint is conscious that towards him God has shown more patience than towards any other mortal; he is not one who boasts that he is not in need of mercy; this would at once class him as a sinner, not as a saint:

> A faithful saying and worthy of all acceptation: that Christ Jesus came into the world to save sinners, of whom I am the chief. But for this cause have I obtained mercy: that in me first Christ Jesus might show forth all patience, for the information of them that shall believe in him unto life everlasting (1 Tim 1:15-16).

Faith in the patience of God is more than an act of humility; it is a positive policy, it is a divine element which has to be taken into account by the ruling powers of the Church, by the leaders of the people of God. If such powers were completely to neglect this aspect of God's dealings with man they would very soon find themselves embarked on deplorable courses, they would jettison good through unwarranted terrors as do men who ignore the craft of seamanship in the hours of tempest; they would readily pronounce all things lost when success was merely deferred.

In reading the history of the Church we ought certainly to make this distinction between the man of God who asks sincerely for reformation and the short-sighted fanatic who, as a self-appointed prophet of woe, denounces all evil. It is not difficult to distinguish between these two categories of rebukers of God's people; there are always those who are ready to command that the fire of heaven should come down, as did the disciples in the days of their ignorance.

One could with profit make the juxtaposition of the passages relating to the Samaritans in the Gospel and in the Acts of the Apostles. In the Gospel narrative the Samaritans close their doors against Jesus and His group of disciples because they "were as men going up to Jerusalem" (Matt 20:18). It is then that the fervent amongst them ask the Lord's leave to command fire to come down from heaven to destroy them. We know the Lord's answer:

> You know not of what spirit you are. The Son of man came not to destroy souls, but to save (Luke 9:55-56).

The scenes related in the Acts about that very city are a contrast full of instruction:

> And Philip, going down to the city of Samaria, preached Christ unto them. And the people with one accord were attentive to those things which were said by Philip, hearing, and seeing the miracles which he did. For many of them who had unclean spirits, crying with a loud voice, went out. And many, taken with the palsy, and that were lame, were healed. There was therefore great joy in that city (Acts 8:5-9).

This no doubt was the sight which Christ had in view when only a few months before He had given that benign answer before the closed gates of that very city.

But this is typical of the people of God at all times and on vaster scales. With infinite patience God prepares the coming generations of fervent believers, bearing with longanimity the men and women of heavy heart and dull understanding who may be the immediate fathers and mothers of a whole nation of saints.

As it would be unpardonable shallowness of thought to leave the Holy Ghost out of count in one's view of the Catholic Church, so it would be a lowering of God's position in the world if one were to visualize the fortunes of the people of God irrespectively of the resources of God's patience towards that people. The patiences of

God belong to the history of that people as much as the doings of the people themselves; the works of the people and the longanimities of God make up that unique history.

✠ 10 ✠

The Religion of the People of God

Although this book is an attempt to describe the spiritual life of the people of God it is indispensable to write separately on the religion of the people of God: Catholic theology is in favor of making this distinction between spiritual life and religion. It is true that, colloquially speaking, the whole range of man's intercourse with God is given the name of religion; but in more exact thought the actual word stands for certain special acts of the higher life differing in tone and quality from the other manifestations of the super natural life. By religion in its specific significance we mean all the deeds of cult, of worship, external and internal, by which we recognize in one way or another the supreme excellence of the Godhead. Religion, we say in theology, is really a part of the virtue of Justice, its highest expression, its most sacred manifestation, making men render unto God the things that are God's.

The acts of religion are as manifold as man's powers of expression: it is practiced with the mind, with the heart, with the tongue, with the hands, with man's whole body, and there is no creature that cannot be utilized and pressed into service for a more complete expression of worship. Through religion living creatures are offered in sacrifice, stones and metals are built into temples and altars, wine and bread are transformed and transubstantiated into highest oblations. The hand of man uses every sort of material in the service of religion, the tongue of man sings the praises of God, the mind and the heart of man meditate on the greatness of God. Religion does all this and much more. The individual man practices it alone, but in its best form religion is exercised by official bodies, by vast agglomerations of believers.

In this matter of religion the Christian differs from the pagan not in degree only but in kind also, because the object of Christian worship is infinitely greater and holier than the object of the pagan cult, and its forms are vastly purer and more expressive. But it is to be admitted, on the other hand, that it is through the special act of religion that there remains amongst all men a certain community of higher life. Unreligious nations are a product of the latter-day apostasy: they are a terrible portent.

The Christian religion is not only the most excellent form of cult and the only true expression of worship, it has moreover this quality, that it is done through charity, through the love of God, so that man renders unto God that which is primarily God's because he loves Him; a feature in religion not known outside the sphere of revelation.

The Christian people, then, are intensely religious because they love the Lord God with their whole heart, their whole mind and their whole strength. Their devotion is informed with piety which is a gift of the Holy Ghost; at no time could the Christian people be religious on a vast scale without possessing a positive love of God. For this has always been the reproach leveled against religion: that men do the deeds of cult whilst their hearts are far from God. We do not pretend that this accusation was never deserved by Christians, yet as a universal historical fact it has to be admitted that Christian worship has always been prompted by love. Christians loved God and they worshipped Him with all the means at their disposal. Still we have to maintain the theological principle that the love of God and the worship of God are two distinct acts, even then when love commands the worship.

Of this worship, then, we speak here and we call it the religion of the people of God. It is indispensable to envisage the works of the people of God from this angle, as it would be otherwise impossible to see in their due proportion many of the manifestations of Catholic activity. Religion is part of the active life of the people of God, in fact it is the highest and most noble form of their activity. In their hearts and in their minds they are filled indeed with the hidden operations of the Spirit, but externally they manifest their love of God, their relationship with God, predominantly through the works of religion.

The practice of religion, it may be said at once, postulates a large amount of externalness; no man is religious merely through internal intercourse with God. That subjection to the divine Majesty which we call religion affects the whole creation through man; in man the world bows before God. So the Christian people have always been most expressive in their religious behavior. Everybody could see their acts of devotion, it was always evident when the Christian world was practicing its religion. Jews and pagans came to know the forms of worship proper to the Christians; if they were out to persecute they knew what to destroy. The emblems of the religion of the people of

God have been carried all over the world; through those emblems one knows, even after the lapse of centuries, whether or not Christ's religion has passed over a given road in the history of the world.

It would most decidedly be a spiritual disaster if Christians were to confine their higher life to internal acts of worship, to mental communications with God. No people of God could exist under such conditions, it must have a voice, it must have a song, it must have an altar, it must have standards, it must have its holy places, it must have its sacred days when with one accord it can proclaim itself for what it is: the people of God.

In this matter I am afraid that at times we Catholics have let the fault-finding of Protestants pass too easily. Let us say it once for all: Protestantism is an effort to establish a Christianity which would not be the people of God, but which would be merely a disconnected selection of independent believers. So, as a consequence, Protestantism has always been very censorious over the forms of religion observed by the people of God in their multitudes: it has given to them the appellation of superstitions. Superstitions there can be amongst Catholics as well as amongst Protestants, just as there can be belief in witchcraft; but an infinitesimal portion only of the religious observances of the people of God would deserve this name of superstition; and then it is never an observance followed by the whole people, but the private aberration of the few.

We ought to bear in mind that the great virtue of religion is a moral virtue, belonging to one of the four cardinal virtues, Justice; it gives to God and to God's saints all the honor that is due to them. Now being a moral virtue it is left to man himself to find the modes for its expression, and is there any province in life in which man is more free than in his methods of declaring esteem and reverence for those that are greater than himself? The fireworks of a Mexican crowd on a festive day can scandalize those only to whom God is a mere abstraction and the saints dead historical personages. But for a people walking by faith in the sight of God and knowing itself to be of the same flesh and blood as the elect who stand before the throne of God, where will be the limit in the method of their jubilation? They will press into service everything that to them means joyousness.

It is said again very often that noisy manifestations of religion are compatible with great ignorance of the doctrines of religion and also with much carelessness in the moral life. Such shortcomings are possible, but it is not because these good folk are ignorant or immoral that they are so boisterous in their religion, it is, on the contrary, their sound remnant of faith and morals that expresses itself so loudly; a downright infidel, a confirmed sinner, will never fire off a gun on the feast-day of the local saint from sheer love of that saint. Quite candidly, there is a vast amount of hypocrisy, not in the external manifestation of Catholic religion, but in the fault-finding attitude of the enemies of Catholicism.

The principal acts of the people of God, right through the centuries, can be easily enumerated: there is first and foremost the Eucharistic Sacrifice; of this we shall speak in a separate chapter. Then there are the sacred days of the people of God, the Sundays and the feasts of the year, the observance of which most unmistakably is the thermometer of the vividness of the faith at any given period. All the Sacraments, besides the Eucharist, may be classed under the heading of religion as they are essentially external deeds through which man professes his dependence on God.

The dedication of men and women to a consecrated service of God is another most constant and universal form of religion in the people of God. We give to that form the appellation of "monastic vows"; the people of God have excelled in this form of religion almost better than in any other.

Then we have the whole region of prayer; the prayer of intercession, the prayer of thanksgiving, the prayer of praise, the prayer of repentance. After that come the more material manifestations of religion: the sacred edifices, the painted pictures and sculptures of heavenly realities, the standard of Christian triumph, the Cross, and the relics of the Saints.

Finally, there are certain corporeal deeds which are definitely acts of divine worship: the castigations of the body, the fasts and abstinences, the bowings and the prostrations before God and His Altar, the signing with the Cross, the marches to the places of sanctity which we call pilgrimages, and even religious dances. In all these things which we only enumerate here in summary fashion, the people of God have always excelled. In the eyes of the world these activities constitute Catholicism, they distinguish the people of God from every other people; by means of these acts there passes right through that mighty body, the Christian people, the sense of oneness and brotherhood. Whoever can do these things is known to be a citizen of that mighty empire.

In days of persecution and oppression those signs of our identity are hidden away, but they are never neglected, much less forgotten; these practices go on in secret fashion and the moment there is the first chance of liberty the people of God stand again ready with all the glorious banners of their supernatural racial life unfurled as of old. Through all the persecutions which the Christian people has had to suffer, not one of the traditional manifestations of religion has been forgotten, has grown strange or become a dead language. There is an amazing similarity in all these matters between Christians of all ages, and there certainly never was a Christian age which did not consider those expressions of religion as absolutely vital to its existence.

In that list we have given of the principal deeds of religion we might well dwell still for a moment on the festive days of the year. The celebration of the Sundays and of the principal liturgical festivities has in the history of the people of God a permanence and a uniformity truly amazing. The Lord's Day is the classical day of repose for the people of God, as the Sabbath was a day of rest for the ancient people. It is only nowadays in Russia that the sacred institution is being attacked, after a similar attempt in the French Revolution had ended in fiasco. Without Sunday the people of God would be without a plan of life; it is the Christian chronology; to abolish Sunday would be to abolish the people of God, because on that day, with its solemn Eucharistic Sacrifice, it asserts its identity.

The great festivals of Christ's Nativity, of Christ's Epiphany, of Christ's Resurrection, of Christ's Ascension, of Christ's sending forth the Spirit of Promise, give to the history of the people of God through all the centuries a oneness that is quite inimitable. We know that every year since the days of the Apostles Christians have assembled for the celebration of those mysteries. Easter has shaped the mentality of the people of God so profoundly that we could hardly think of such a people without its Easter. All generations of Christians give each other their hands in their Common celebration of the Easter mystery. The people of God is essentially an Easter people and so it will remain until the Lord come.

One is always reluctant to speak of any institution, even inside the Catholic Church, as being directly of divine origin; we know, of course, quite clearly that certain acts in the life of the Catholic

Church are divinely ordered and appointed things, as, for instance, the celebration of the Eucharistic Sacrifice and the administration of the Sacraments. When one considers, however, the supreme role which the main liturgical feasts of the Church have played in the shaping of the character of the people of God, one is inclined to think that those feasts are of divine institution, that they are part and parcel of the Christian economy of life. It is certain that the powers of darkness more than ever identify the abolition of Christianity with the abolition of the Christian feasts. There can be no doubt as to the necessity of those festivities for the prosperity of the people of God.

If it were objected that the Catholic feast is mainly an aesthetical factor in Christian life, the objection would in no wise diminish the profound importance of the celebration; the aesthetical elements in the life of a people are absolutely indispensable to the people's power. But if the poetry of the feast be at the same time truest dogma, then the cessation of the feast will mean a catastrophe beyond repair. So for all practical purposes a world without an Easter would be a godless world, it would be a world in which Satan had triumphed. *Beatus populus, qui scit jubilationem.* "Blessed indeed is the people that knows how to praise" (Ps 88:16).

This blessing has been without ceasing the proper quality of the people of God; when the people are free they indulge themselves in that blessedness to their heart's content, and when the hand of persecution is heavy on them they suffer from an ineradicable nostalgia for the Canticles of Zion.

✠ 11 ✠

The Divine Latitudes

The expression "latitude" applied to the dealings of God with His people may appear ill-chosen to many a reader. Has not this word become unholy through being applied to that state of religious mind which does not want to submit to definite limits and rules? Latitudinarianism is not a commendable frame of mind. Yet it seems to me that in God's dealings with His people there is a feature which can hardly be described otherwise than by making use of this very word latitude. Latitude, of course, means breadth; but the Latin form has a nuance which is not found in the Saxon vocable. There is in the notion of latitude an element of far reaching attentiveness which is not contained in the simple idea of breadth. God takes interest in realities which to the human mind appear hardly worthy of the attention of the divine Majesty.

The Scriptures, and above all, the Psalms, are redolent of that atmosphere of divine latitude; the young raven in his nest is said to cry to God for his food and the lion's whelp in pursuit of his prey, pouncing and roaring, is also said to be seeking his meat from the hand of God. A divinity that was indifferent to life in its lower forms would not be an infinite divinity, it would merely be a finite potentate. A god who was not the god of the little ones, who was not the maker of what is small and tiny would not be a creator in the true sense. The great mystics of Catholicism have always reveled in God's power to do the small things, in God's love for the least fragment of created reality; in the words of the Scriptures:

> God will not accept any man's person, neither will he stand in awe of any man's greatness: for he made the little and the great, and he hath equally care of all (Wis 6:8).

It is not contrary to Christian teaching to say that God is the author of the weak things of the earth, that He definitely wants many things to be weak so that His power may be made manifest:

> Jesus answered: Neither hath this man sinned, nor his parents; but that the works of God should be made manifest in him (John 9:3).

These words were spoken by the Son of God over the man who had been born blind; the disciples at the sight of this human misery had given utterance to their racial prejudice, either this man or his parents had sinned that he should be born blind. There is in this remark a lack of logic which emphasizes the purely human reading of human events. The unborn man could not have sinned as he had as yet no existence, but no doubt those good Israelites found it less difficult to credit with hypothetical sinfulness a human being than to admit that God Himself might in a way be responsible for allowing his imperfection. We may suppose that they had some sort of theology according to which God was foreseeing the future sins of that man and struck him with blindness from his birth in anticipation of the coming guilt. But their own holy books could have told them that the deeper Judaic wisdom was not against God's permissive authorship of human infirmity, as God also seeks to be considered in the light of the supreme and merciful physician.

In Ecclesiasticus we have a truly delightful elaboration of this gift of the divine latitude in the praise of every kind of human occupation which is necessary for the well-being of a city; all crafts belong, according to the inspired text, to the divine ordering of things:

> The wisdom of a scribe cometh by his time of leisure: and he that is less in action shall receive wisdom. With what wisdom shall he be furnished that holdeth the plough and that glorieth in the goad, that driveth the oxen therewith, and is occupied in their labors: and his whole talk is about the offspring of bulls? He shall give his mind to turn up furrows: and his care is to give the kine fodder (Eccl 38:25-27).

The craftsman who makes the brazen seal, the smith standing by the anvil, in whose ears there is always the noise of the hammer, the potter sitting at his work and turning the wheel, all these have their activities described lovingly by the divine author; the importance of their existence is summed up in the words "Without these a city is not built" (Eccl 38:32) It is true that they are not the governing body: "Upon the judge's seat they shall not sit" (Eccl 38:34), yet they are men of power:

> They shall strengthen the state of the world: and their prayer shall be in the work of their craft, applying their soul, and searching in the law of the most High (Eccl 38:39).

We say quite naturally that this is the ideal Of a Christian people and we are right in saying so. It is the permanently divine ideal valid at all times; it is faith in God's presence; it is faith in man's nobility; it is that sense of perfect proportion that makes every man realize to how great an extent he depends on the good will and the labors of his fellow-men. No state can be built up without the contribution of the busy hands of the millions, but everyone in that crowd is in immediate contact with God through the supernatural life, "applying his soul to God and searching in the law of the most High."

If Catholic spirituality at any time were devoid of sympathy for the burdens of the life of the poor, it would stand self condemned as an illusion, as a pride of the spirit. Even in its highest aspect Catholic spirituality is in immediate contact with the simplicities, the domesticities, not to say the vulgarities, of the human crowds, because the crowds are God's dear creatures; He has given them that condition of life, He endows them with graces and instincts and perceptions that enable them to fulfill their destiny. The Catholic theologian, with all he knows about divine grace, is the one man who ought to be perfectly at ease in the seething human crowds who ask for bread but who also, in their own way, ask for God and for His Christ.

Though we love to find among Christians the gift of heroicity in the practice of their faith, we love the people of God too well to withdraw our measure of praise even from the humblest effort at following Christ: "Not minding high things but consenting to the humble" (Rom 12:16) is an exquisite precept known only to Christianity. There are occasions everywhere for us to practice it; we must be content to be fellow Christians, nay, even fellow-workers with many a weaker brother. We must bear the burdens of those who are less strong than ourselves. No people can be made up exclusively of strong and brave men; even a spiritual people cannot aspire to such perfection. It is invariably the maker of sects who is exacting beyond human endurance. It would almost seem as if he tried to find compensation for his apostasy from dogmatic faith in some prodigious human virtue. Those whose faith is strong, whose understanding of the mysteries of God's mercy is of a high order, can easily reconcile it with their high ideals that there should be in practice so many weak souls who are saved chiefly by the happy fact that they are carried forward in the ranks of their braver fellow-soldiers.

✠ 12 ✠

The Divine Interventions

Nothing is more evident in the career of the ancient people of God than the constant interventions of the divine power in shaping the fortunes of that people. We must, of course, take the Biblical view of the history of Israel, not the interpretations of the modern archaeologist who sees no more in the vicissitudes of the Jewish nation than the play of political powers. God was constantly raising His people and He was as persistently humbling them for their infidelities.

Is there on the part of God an equal vigilance over the fortunes of the new people, so that inspired writers could write its history, so immensely more marvellous than the account of God's first people? We know the promises which Christ has made to His Church; we are familiarized with the doctrine of the Church's indefectibility and infallibility; we know that through a very special supernatural providence the Church will always remain true to Christ's ideal and that she will not be overcome by the powers of darkness: the gates of hell shall not prevail against her. But it would hardly be in keeping with all we know about the ways of God if the divine intervention under the new dispensation had to be limited to a mere preservation, to a protective act which would just save the life of the Church. There must be endless interventions on the part of God in the course followed by the new people if the ancient prototype of Israel is to be of any guidance to us.

It is precisely in this matter that we see the advantage of completing the notion of "Church" with the subsidiary idea of "people." It sounds really better to speak of a people with whom God in turns is either pleased or angry, than to apply to the Church herself those varieties in divine behavior. We feel less reluctant to say that the people of God are being punished for their sins than that the Church is castigated for her infidelities; it is less offensive to our ears to hear a people being rebuked for their scandals by the inspired and authorized preachers, than to listen to the denunciations of an unworthy Church.

We know, of course, that radically the notions of Church and people are conterminous; at the same time if we can apply to the Church all the features that belong to a people it will be easier for us to keep the distinction between the divine and the human in Christ's institution. Moreover, the method that has prevailed for so long of scolding the Church directly has led to the impression that churchmen properly so-called, that is to say ecclesiastics, have been the only sinners, when after all the Catholic of the lay communion has been as unworthy of his calling as the cleric. Let us see in both clergy and laity one people who live in that house of God, the Church, and who behave either as worthy or as unworthy servants. It is thus Christ seems to view the future behaviour of those that were to bear His Name. They are servants in His house, of all degrees, doing every kind of work and also differing greatly in conduct. There are those who watch and are ready to receive Him on His return; there are those who say in their hearts, "My lord is long a-coming" (Mark 24:48), and their false liberty soon degenerates into license.

We may, then, for all practical purposes apply to the Christian people whatever we know of the ways of God with the ancient people, with, however, this difference, that more than ever God will show Himself rich in patience and mercies towards His people; He will forgive them because in the midst of them is the great mystery of propitiation, the Sacrifice of Christ; He will have patience with them because in the new people the prayer for forgiveness is an unending stream that flows broad and deep; He will spare the people because the conditions are immensely happier than in the days of Abraham, as the number of the just amongst the sinners is at all times extremely imposing.

This, of course, does not mean that God is never angered with His people; one of the great invocations on the lips of Christians is this: *Ab ira tua libera nos, Domine*, "From thy wrath deliver us, O Lord." There is, according to St. Peter, reason for even God's own to tremble:

> For the time is that judgment should begin at the house of God. And if first at us, what shall be the end of them that believe not the gospel of God? And if the just man shall scarcely be saved, where shall the ungodly and the sinner appear (1 Pet 4:17-18)?

There is no telling how severe the judgements of God may be in this life on those of His own household; the sufferings of Catholic nations in the past and also at the present hour are a scandal to many.

They see no sign of special divine favor in the fortunes of genuinely Christian states, indeed, the fate that befalls the Catholic peoples is in lurid contrast to the apparently happier circumstances of kingdoms that have repudiated the Faith. Thus in the past, idolatrous Egypt or corrupt Babylon may have despised, in the pride of their power, poor down-trodden Israel; yet neither Egypt nor Babylon exists today, while Israel is still an immense power in the world.

To be God's people is a terrible privilege because it means that divine measures, not human measures, are applied to it. Duration of time seems to be the one factor that counts least in God's dealings as He is so sure of the future; so for long centuries the people of God may be made to sail on a sea of tribulation before they are granted the omnipotent breeze of success. But of one thing we may be absolutely certain; at no time does God abandon His people. Not only does He not desert His Church, but He is with His people as He was with Israel, giving them constantly fresh pastures, new openings, replenishing their deficiencies, filling up again the measure of their vitalities. He raises great men, not only of the directly spiritual plane, but of every order; great Catholic kings as well as great Popes, artists as well as doctors, great soldiers as well as founders of Orders; He gives His people prosperity and even wealth; He puts into their hands new means to subdue the world, for it is not only graces we receive, but every good gift and best gift comes from the Father of light.

We ought to remember that the conditions of existence of the people of God are not exclusively human; they are surrounded by the dark powers of evil, the fallen angels whose constant aim it is to make them unhappy, for Satan is the hater of man. True, it is his final purpose to destroy the Church, but he does evil for the sake of evil; he takes pleasure in human misery; he is the enemy of the human race out of an incomprehensible jealousy. So he is incessantly at work to harm the people of God not only in their souls, but also in their bodies, not only in their faith but also in their temporal possessions; he loathes beauty, he abominates the joy of innocent life, he is tormented by the peace of men; to disturb the people of God is his joy. Thus the saints have always viewed Satan not only as a tempter, but also as a doer of evil for evil's sake.

Against this ill-will of a countless army of spirits the Christian people would have no chance unless there were over them the unceasing protection of their Lord and King; unremittingly God must intervene to undo the evil which His enemy has done. It would not be possible for the people of God to carry on with the gifts received at the beginning, very soon such reserves would be exhausted; new providences, new interventions on the part of God are necessary at every hour.

It is in this matter that the wisdom and the patience of the saints show themselves; to await the turn of events is an extremely wise attitude; in other words, over and over again there are happenings in the political and in the physical world whose bearing on the fortunes of the people of God are simply incalculable; apparently those events are entirely human both in their origin and in their execution. Yet very soon it becomes manifest that they are the direct causes of tremendous transformations in the conditions of the people of God. God has intervened through the acts of man. Of God it is said constantly in the liturgy of the Church that He makes use of evil men and evil deeds to bring about His marvellous works.

All the strength at the disposal of the people of God could not have done one portion of the good that has been wrought by agencies completely outside the control of the people. Thus the breaking-down of the pagan Roman Empire in the vision of St. John is applauded in heaven as the triumph of the Lamb, as the avenging of the blood of the martyrs. If a Christian army had gone forth and had broken the great pagan power the sense of triumph could not have been more overpowering. But it was not Christian soldiers who did the work, it was done by the hordes of the northern barbarians. This was God's intervention in favor of His people and we know what this meant for the future development of Christianity.

On a smaller scale, but equally interesting, we have the fortunes of the Catholics in England ; the great liberty of today is only exceeded in impressiveness by the terrors of the long years and centuries of the penal laws. Now who brought about that change? Was it any concerted action of the sparse Catholic population of these islands? We know, of course, that it was not so. A number of political events, chief of them the Napoleonic Wars, brought about the period of toleration to which we have become so habituated that we can hardly think of any other mode of existence.

So one might multiply the marvels of divine intervention. As it is said in Hosea:

> I will have mercy on the house of Judah and I will save them by the Lord their God: and I will not save them by bow, nor by sword, nor by battle, nor by horses, nor by horsemen (Hos 1:7).

The meaning of the prophet is not that no war like apparatus will be used by God Almighty to bring about His people's salvation. Wars there will be; but it is not His people who will go to war, the nations around them will be warring against each other and the final result will be the salvation of Israel, almost without cost to themselves.

✠ 13 ✠

The Supplications of the People of God

We may take it for granted that a form of supplication which would suit the needs of a whole people at all times, under all circumstances, could not be formulated by the genius of man; the duties, the rights and the needs of a people are so vast that no mind except one that can survey the people from end to end could express in a short prayer all the intercessory activity of that people.

The Lord's Prayer is preeminently the prayer of the people of God. As its originator is the Son of God Himself, we need feel no surprise at its character; it is, indeed, a supplication which a whole people could utter with one voice at the same time, and not one of its petitions is either too high in its aims, or too sweeping in its demands, or, on the other hand, too narrow to suit multitudes whom no man could number. The Our Father is in very truth the prayer of a people, at all times, under every possible variety of circumstance and of fortune.

Perhaps it might be possible, with the modern inventions of bringing people together not only in hearing but in speaking, to organize national recitals of the Lord's Prayer; it would be seen then how the prayer which Christ gave is a supreme prayer in the sense that all men can pray it and that its demands are about matters which are perpetually with us; nor could any man ask for greater things than those contained in the petitions of that prayer which all men can say together without falseness or hypocrisy. If there were a vast assembly of a hundred million believers, with one mouth, and with one mind, they could recite together that prayer and no man would need to feel that words were put upon his lips which meant nothing to him.

The nearest realization to such a spectacle in the writer's experience was the great moment of the Eucharistic Congress at Dublin when, as is commonly admitted, a million Irishmen assisted at the great Mass in Phoenix Park. By means of loud speakers the words of the *Pater* of the Mass were brought home to every man in that immense congregation, and knowing as we do the temper of that multitude of fervent believers we may take it for granted that they all made their own the words that came to them from the celebrant at the Altar.

It is precisely this universality of contents that makes the *Pater* what it is, that makes it the national supplication of the people of God. Innumerable books have been written by good and wise men of all degrees upon it; its contents are inexhaustible. My intention here is only this: to bring out that character of universality which makes of it essentially the perfect supplication of a whole people in its millions.

The Lord's Prayer supposes in him who utters it a spiritual outlook, a condition of existence, a disposition of heart that is possible to every man; it is not the prayer of the few, of the privileged. The man who says the Our Father takes for granted the sovereignty and the primacy of God; God's interests are his first concern, and God's interests in their widest sense, not in any transitory form of passing actuality. He who prays thus is conscious of the real needs of humanity; the double need of food and forgiveness. He knows that the human race is constitutionally exposed to dangers and that God only can avert the perils 'that come from the race itself and from the spiritual enemies of the race; he feels deeply the presence of evil.

But with all that consciousness of sin and evil he is also aware of his own share in making all things right again. He makes a promise in the very midst of his supplication which, in a mysterious way, constitutes him the partner of God; he undertakes to forgive as he is being forgiven, an undertaking that is in the power of every human being and for which in practice there is an occasion in the heart of every man. God is addressed by the Name that is the most comprehensive, "Our Father who art in heaven." All particularism is excluded by the very terms of that invocation:

> And if you invoke as Father him who, without respect of persons, judgeth according to every one's work: converse in fear during the time of your sojourning here (1 Pet 1:17).

The first three petitions are an admirable expression of the ultimate aim of the people of God:

> Hallowed by thy name; thy kingdom come; thy will be done on earth as it is in heaven (Matt 6:9).

The glorification of God's Name is the people's supreme ambition; this act gives the people its proper character of being theocentric in all its aspirations, for it has no more doubt about the need of praising God than an earthly nation has about the necessity of defending its frontiers. It stands and it falls by the glory of God. This glory is its pride, its security, its peace, because it knows that in its essentials it cannot be thwarted. But let us remember that the glory of God is an object of prayer, of supplication; it is a work that has to be carried out, a favor that has to be granted, a gift that has to be bestowed on the people of God. At no time is the people happier than when God rises in His might and compels all men to adore Him: these are the days of triumph for God's people. It is not concerned directly with its own successes; a glorious God, manifested to the eyes of men, is the supreme happiness for which it hungers and thirsts and therefore its first petition is for that very thing: that the Name of the Lord should be on the tongues of all men.

The coming of the kingdom of heaven, which is the second petition, is the same thing as the confirmation of the people of God in all its rights and privileges besides new conquests of the faith. The prayer for the coming of the kingdom is not the expectation of a happy state of things not yet existing, it is like the prayer for the coming of the Holy Ghost, it means the extension of a power already existing, the furtherance of a cause already firmly established. When the people of God intercedes for the kingdom of God it is not like men in exile who cry out for the favor of repatriation; it is more like men who petition their sovereign to lead them to fresh conquests and new enterprises.

The third petition, as we ought to remember, is not primarily an act of resignation to the will of God; it is like all the other petitions of the *Pater*, directly and essentially a request. We pray that God in His omnipotence may overcome on this earth all obstacles to His holy will as He has overcome them in heaven. We may see in this petition an allusion to the fall of the angels; we may hear in it an echo of the great battle that took place in heaven when the will of God obtained that supreme triumph, when all rebellious wills were cast out; when Satan, the great adversary of God, fell from heaven like lightning: for such a triumph we pray, for on this earth there are still many wills that are in opposition to God, the wills of the evil spirits and the wills of sinful men:

> And there was a great battle in heaven: Michael and his angels fought with the dragon, and the dragon fought, and his angels. And they prevailed not: neither was their place found any more in heaven. And that great dragon was cast out, that old serpent, who is called the devil and Satan, who seduceth the whole world. And he was cast unto the earth: and his angels were thrown down with him. And I heard a loud voice in heaven, saying: Now is come salvation and strength and the kingdom of our God and the power of His Christ: because the accuser of our brethren is cast forth, who accused them before our God day and night. And they overcame him by the blood of the Lamb and by the word of the testimony: and they loved not their lives unto death. Therefore, rejoice, O heavens, and you that dwell therein. Woe to the earth and to the sea, because the devil is come down unto you, having great wrath, knowing that he hath but a short time. And when the dragon saw that he was cast unto the earth, he persecuted the woman who brought forth the man child (Rev 12:7-13).

Could there be a petition worthier of a mighty people than this demand that God's will should be supreme on earth as it is now in heaven? It is truly a battle cry as well as a supplication: it means the martialing of all the forces that are on God's side against the evil powers whose will is in a state of rebellion. With fear and trembling the people over and over again repeat the words of this mysterious intercession; they know that the demand cannot be granted without the destruction of all the high things that stand up against God:

> For the weapons of our warfare are not carnal but mighty to God, unto the pulling down of fortifications, destroying counsels, and every height that exalteth itself against the knowledge of God: and bringing into captivity every understanding unto the obedience of Christ: and having in readiness to revenge all disobedience, when your obedience shall be fulfilled (2 Cor 10:4-6).

In praying this great prayer the people implicitly submit to all the hardships of that warfare, they know that the balance of divine justice, which is God's will, cannot be reestablished without repentance, without man giving satisfaction unto God. So although the third petition be directly a postulation it is also a cry of resignation under the mighty hand of God in the day of visitation; for this is one of the most pleasing features in the character of the people of God, that they submit without murmuring even to the harsh and hard ordinances of divine providence because through them very often God carries out His blessed will, and brings about the ultimate victory of the divine kingdom. Nothing would be more contrary to the true temper of that people than insistence on uninterrupted successfulness in all undertakings. It is good for the people to be humbled and to learn its dependence on God.

The prayer which Christ gave to His people is not the prayer of angels; it is the prayer of men whose life depends on the fertility of the earth. The economic concerns of God's family are not neglected or overlooked, they affect life too profoundly to be left out of sight; there is no false idealism, there is no impossible other-worldliness in the people, they carry out their work on this earth and from this earth they must live; their daily bread is the end of their external physical activities, of their labors, not in the sense that they labour not for the higher life, but that the work in the sweat of the brow which is the condition of man here on earth is the finding of the food for the human multitudes. And yet though they labour hard for the food, when the bread does come it is the gift of God because innumerable are the remote causes, besides the effort of man, which make or mar the harvests of the earth.

So the Christian people make of the mighty economic problem a prayer; they ask for bread as they ask for grace, because in the last instance the nourishing of the human race is dependent on causes which are the free dispositions of the Father who is in heaven. Just as hunger is the most elemental of all human evils, a catastrophe that will break the stoutest heart and dissolve the mightiest armies, so is the gift of bread the great means which God has to rally all men round His seat of majesty; expecting their bread from God, men are united with God; to eat the food from the hand of God is essentially communion with God, and could there be anything more touching than to hear a whole people speak in confidence and faith the simple words, "Give us this day our daily bread"?

The trust with which the people of God pray this prayer constitutes their true economic Wealth; through all the vicissitudes of possessions, of activities, the ultimate and the elemental reality will always be the feeding of the people. Christ put on our lips, not a prayer for the means, but a prayer for the end; we are not asking for riches which are the means towards the nourishment of the human race, we are asking for the very end, that all the children of God be satiated every day. Various are the means, but one is the end, and such is the confidence of that prayer that even an extra providence would step in if the ordinary means to feed the human race were to fail.

The sins of the people do not destroy the people as long as there is the cry for pardon. All the guilt that may be in the consciences of millions of free agents is put in this one demand, "Forgive us our trespasses." There is no exception; there is no crime so heinous as to be excluded; it is the people's indebtedness to God, and unhesitatingly the people asks that the debt be remitted to the last farthing.

The divine truthfulness of the prayer is revealed in this petition with amazing clarity. The supplicants themselves, of their own accord, strike a bargain with God; they also in their turn will forgive everything, personal wrongs, national wrongs; there is no wrong so exorbitant as not to be made the object of that bargain between God and man. Here again we may see the incomprehensibly great implications of those simple petitions when we think of them as being uttered by a whole people. What a prodigious transformation it would mean if sincerely, from the bottom of their heart, the millions who say the prayer together forgave everything that makes them suffer.

It is at this point that one almost Wonders whether the Our Father is not a prayer too high for human conditions. But let us remember that it is the prayer of the people of God and it presupposes that charity which is poured out in the hearts of men through the Holy Ghost. A pagan nation, an apostate people could not pray thus, because revenge, not forgiveness is their code of honor. Could we not say that this petition of the *Pater* is the dividing line between a Christian and a non-Christian people? To make such a pact with God is unthinkable in the case of the nations who boast in the glory of their material power and whose whole ideal is self-exaltation.

The conditions of existence of the people of God have already been hinted at in the words of St. John's Revelation, when the great dragon is described as having taken up his abode on this earth; the mysterious struggle between God and His adversary goes on and the struggle is not a personal encounter between God and Satan, but the battle takes place within the boundaries of the people. We ask then that in this mighty contest We be spared the dangers of a conflict almost too acute for human forces; we ask for our captain, God, to make easy for us the conditions of that warfare, not to lead us into dangerous places, to remember our weakness, to protect us from the surprises of an enemy who is extremely cunning. In other words our demand is this: that the spiritual warfare be mitigated in our favor, that we be spared the whole brunt of the hostile attack. For though we be a brave and loyal people we are not spirits fighting spirits, we have not the rapid thought and clear vision of those ancient armies of God, the angels; we are easily deceived and ensnared, and although we are ready to die in the good fight we are fearful lest we should be overreached by an immensely clever enemy.

We ask not to be led into temptation and we ask also to be freed from all contact with the evil one, from the power of Satan, from the slavedom of sin; for this is the deplorable condition of the world at large, that it has been ensnared by Satan, by the old serpent, by the great seducer, by the father of lies. We cry to God to liberate us, to deliver us from all evil, as a small nation, say, would pray that it be delivered from the grasp of some sinister political power that surrounds it on all sides; though the small nation be free so far, the danger of losing its liberty is an imminent danger. It is in this sense that the people of God pray to be delivered from evil; they themselves are not slaves, they are free, but everywhere else the power of Satan is uncontested; the very vicinity of that dark slavedom makes us cry to God to keep us free.

It ought to be evident to all of us that this divine supplication, the Lord's Prayer, is always heard whenever the Christian utters it with faith and confidence, for the objects of those mighty demands are the very purposes which God has in view. At every Pater that is whispered or sung, each one of the seven petitions is furthered, is nearer fulfillment, for there can be no obstacle to such an advance as the favor demanded transcends individual worthiness or unworthiness; the whole people is benefited and the good things which are asked for and the evil from which an escape is prayed for, transcend all local circumstances.

The transaction of that prayer is truly a national transaction; it is of the nature of a universal compact with God. Let us be certain then that not one of our *Paters* ever falls to the ground, that forevery one of them the kingdom of God is advanced, the power of evil is diminished, and some human hunger is stilled; literally with this prayer Christ's words come true:

> You have not chosen me: but I have chosen you; and have appointed you, that you should go and should bring forth fruit; and your fruit should remain: that whatsoever you shall ask of the Father in my name, he may give it you (John 15:16).

✠ 14 ✠

THE POPULAR ASPECT OF THE DIVINE GIFTS

THERE IS, I THINK, A GREAT GAIN TOWARDS OUR UNDERstanding of the Christian mysteries in our willingness to look upon those mysteries as being instituted, not for an *élite*, but for a people. In the ordinary concerns of human life we know at once what is meant when it is said that some event is intended for the people, that a festivity or a work or an institution is intended for the people. Let us, for the sake of clearness, think of some festive occasion in which the people in their multitudes are invited to take part; there will be as we all know an elemental character in the program of such a day if it is to be a success. The cause of the feast, its meaning and its arrangements will be such that even the most unsophisticated and the most primitive of the nation's children will be able to enter into it whole-heartedly.

Human society has been divided, not unnaturally, into aristocracy and democracy; very different are the interests of those two sections of the social order. This analogy of democracy and aristocracy is helpful here, in order to bring out a very important aspect of God's dealings with men. Even in the highest sphere, in the supernatural sphere, it may be said universally that all the provisions made by God for the elevation of mankind have this popular character: they are essentially the feasts of a whole people, the duties of a whole people, the sentiments and the ideals of a whole people, not the interests merely of a refined and educated class or aristocracy. Christianity, in other words, is the religion of a people, and there is nothing official in Christianity that has not this democratic characteristic of being within the reach of every member of the Christian society.

Any exclusivism in the distribution of the good things of Christianity is an abomination in the eyes of God. Christ denounced the scribes and Pharisees because they kept to themselves the key of knowledge, they did not enter themselves into the kingdom of God and they prevented others from entering in; they had made of religion the privilege of a class. Christ, the Son of God, at every turn shows how for Him the kingdom of God is presented to everyone, to the publican, to the sinner, to the harlot, to the thief, to the child, to all without exception. As we know, the Pharisees were greatly scandalized at this attitude of Jesus of Nazareth, apparently so little aristocratic. In the Gospel we have this divine popularity brought out most forcibly.

If at any time our view of Christianity were tainted with a pretense of privilege, if we appreciated only certain high manifestations of the mystical life, we should be really in danger of falling under Christ's curse against the Pharisees. Christ and His religion are not for the classes but for the masses, and everything in the divine dispensation of the new Law has this characteristic of being the religion of the masses, the higher life of a whole people.

This point of view is brought out very forcibly in the Catholic theology of the sacraments. I do not say that it is only the sacraments that possess this feature of being directly the concern of the masses—everything in Christianity, in dogma as well as in practice, is meant for the human multitude—but in the sacraments as the Catholic Church administers them we have an exceptionally clear corroboration of this point of view; there is not one of the seven sacraments which by its very nature is anything but a spiritual provision made for a multitude; they are essentially given to a whole people. There is in the sacramental theology a positive recoil from any spiritual exclusivism; one might almost say that a sacrament would revolt against class appropriation; it would be a desecration of a sacrament, not a veneration of it, if it were restricted to a chosen portion of men.

Nothing, of course, is easier than to apply these views to every one of those seven divine institutions. To begin with, the sacrament of new birth, Holy Baptism; Christ announces it in terms of astonishing universality: "Go ye and baptize all nations" (Matt 28:19). The water of baptism is found everywhere, all men can baptize, all men can be baptized. Baptism is not the initiation of a few into a recondite mystery; it is the washing of multitudes on the seashore, on the banks of rivers, in the large baptisteries of the early Church. Faith in Christ is the one condition necessary. To the eye of the saint there could be nothing more marvelous than to see a crowd of human beings, thrown together as by chance, being baptized in the Name of the Father and the Son and the Holy Ghost. The plebeian aspect of it all is what rejoices the heart of those to whom it is given to understand the mystery of the kingdom of God.

The Catholic practice of baptizing infants is one of those spiritual facts which have ramifications into practically every branch of theology. There is, however, a preeminent appropriateness in infant baptism if we consider all those who are called by God unto Christ as a people; baptism is the birth of that people, and every people begins with the law of birth, with the delicate powers of childhood; our little ones are as dear to us in the supernatural sense as they are in the ordinary human order; they are the hope of the people of God, they occupy a large place in the fortunes of the people of God; their growth and their upbringing is the gravest concern of the people of God.

The Catholic feeling always has been this, to give to the children the full faith of Christ, to let them enter into it, not with precaution and trembling, but with joyfulness and even boisterousness. A people, unless its mentality be warped by false social principles, will give to childhood a full life, a natural and spontaneous development; the children share in the tradition and the wealth of a nation from the moment of their birth, without ceasing. So with the people of God there is no real problem of childhood; the supernatural is the ordinary condition in which those children live and they become the people of God as men and women through a most sweet and healthy progression. Many errors would be avoided, both in theory and practice, if we could bring ourselves to accept habitually this view, that Christian baptism for the offspring of Christians is a true birth of a people, not only a recondite and remote means of justification.

The Christian child has the rights of the Christian people; to take away any of his joy in believing is a great crime. We know Christ's Words concerning the little ones that believe in Him, that if any man should scandalize one such it would be better for him to have a millstone hung round his neck and be drowned in the depths of the sea. Christ's words are as significant as they are touching. He speaks of the little ones that believe in Him; this is the traditional Catholic sentiment, that His children from their tenderest years have the fullness of faith; the supernatural order of things, in old Christian parlance, has come to them with their mother's milk; Christian motherhood is seen in its true proportions then only if we know that truly on this earth there is the people of God whose life and propagation is the glory and the dignity of the Christian mother.

The sacrament of the chrism for a long time now has been administered almost invariably to large crowds of *confirmandi*. It is the growing boy and the growing girl who come to the bishop in their hundreds and their thousands to be anointed with the chrism, to be strengthened in the spirit, to be signed as soldiers of Christ. The most obvious counterpart in ordinary national life is the swearing in of the young recruit.

Sometimes one may hear voices of well-meaning men asking for a more individual and exclusive administration of the sacrament of Confirmation; they seem to dread the openness, nay even the vulgarity of the large gatherings of youths from all parts on Confirmation days. But here again if we go back to the purest tradition we find that the Spirit almost invariably comes down on crowds, on hundreds and thousands assembled together. At His first coming His advent was manifest; He descended on a hundred and twenty souls. The multitudes of our young ones thronging round their bishops is really a more traditional event than the almost secret administration of the sacrament to the convert of more intellectual standard.

The soldiers of the people of God are being enrolled; in fact, every Christian is proclaimed to be a soldier, the Christian people are a people of soldiers and the Holy Ghost is a mighty Spirit that animates the whole nation. The people of God are the people of the

Spirit; their instincts, their courage, their tastes, their temperaments as a people come from the Spirit; they all receive the sacrament of the chrism. In the power of the Spirit, according to Ezekiel's vision, they all stand on their feet as an army exceedingly great.

How different is the practical Catholic view of the Spirit and His coming to men from those well-intentioned but distinctly erroneous spirit-religions of which England, for instance, has produced several varieties! The spirit whom the Quaker expects is not the spirit of the whole people, it is the spirit of a chosen assembly; the Catholic Church, on the contrary, expects the Spirit to animate every one of her children, to seal every one of the souls that have the faith of Christ, to become, in every member of the supernatural people, at least a potential source of higher life.

Catholicism has always avoided making Confirmation the privilege of the few or the recompense of those that are already advanced in the school of Christian education; practically the Church takes this line of conduct, that with the growing years her children are in need of greater supernatural powers; so she insists on all those being confirmed in the Spirit who reach the age of puberty. She treats the question, one might say, nationally; she has her age limit for presenting her children to the Spirit.

With the Bread of Life, we enter at once into the midst of a vast people, into crowds before whom are worked the wonders that symbolize it, to whom it is first announced, to whom it is given ultimately. Everything in the Eucharist is in terms of a multitude, of a people. The multiplication of the bread and of the fishes in the wilderness was the one great miracle that symbolized the coming of the Eucharist, through that sign Christ fed five thousand men, not counting the women and the children:

THE POPULAR ASPECT OF THE DIVINE GIFTS 111

When Jesus therefore had lifted up his eyes and seen that a very great multitude cometh to him, he said to Philip: Whence shall we buy bread, that these may eat? ... Philip answered him: Two hundred pennyworth of bread is not sufficient for them, that every one may take a little (John 6:5-7).

Was the sum of two hundred pennies the greatest financial figure to which the simple-minded disciple was accustomed? Not a purse of two hundred pence but the power of Moses who gave bread from heaven would have been equal to the occasion. The evangelists delight in giving the size of that crowd and the description of its picturesqueness:

And he (Christ) commanded them that they should make them all sit down by companies upon the green grass, and they sat down in ranks, by hundreds and by fifties (Mark 6:39-40).

For none of His miracles did the Son of God prepare such a perfect setting of expectant humanity; He had in front of Him a people. When they had eaten and when they realized the greatness of the sign that had taken place they became a political power; they spoke amongst themselves; they felt that Christ was with them and they were on the point of rising as one man to make Him into their king when He fled from them alone into the mountains.

It is again to the multitude that He announces the mystery of the bread that comes down from heaven, the secret of His Flesh and of His Blood. The new saying, which many found so hard, was couched in comprehensive terms for popular interest:

This is the bread which cometh down from heaven: that if any man eat of it, he may not die (John 6:50).

The ancient people had eaten the manna; it was the everlasting glory of the Jewish nation to have been fed by God miraculously; the new people are immensely more privileged:

> This is the bread that came down from heaven. Not as your fathers did eat manna and are dead. He that eateth this bread shall live forever (John 6:59).

Their Bread will be the Flesh of the Son of Man, their drink will be His Blood, but though infinitely holier than the manna that came from heaven its distribution is much vaster than was the distribution of the manna of the desert; this new manna will fall on the surface of the whole earth because the new people will be found everywhere: "And the bread that I will give is my flesh, for the life of the world" (John 6:52).

The extent of the distribution of the Eucharistic Bread may at times scandalize the narrow-minded who forget that the Father who sends the Bread thinks in terms of a people; He feeds a people as He feeds all living creatures. In the Eucharistic liturgy the Church applies to the heavenly Bread all the utterances of the inspired Writers concerning the natural bread. Those vast terms are the only relevant ones; a whole nation eat the fruit of their labor, the product of their soil; a whole people, the people of God, eat the Bread of God, the Body of Christ, of which faith and fidelity to God make them worthy.

We all know of controversies about the frequency of sacramental communion amongst Christians; in this matter as in many others, men had forgotten that the Bread of angels had become the Bread of men, that it had become the Bread of a people; they thought it was a delicacy reserved for the rich in spirit, for the few: this controversy was on the point of becoming one of the most dangerous heresies. At bottom, pride was the cause of this theological perversion: men came to consider Christian life to be the achievement of the few only and consequently the Bread of God was not for the masses but for the *élite*. The communion of the children as well as the baptism of infants is a practice that presupposes an understanding of God's dealing with souls which could easily be lost had we not the official guidance of the Church, if we had not saintly spirits who see things in the light of God. The Pope of the people, Pius X, was one of those saintly ones raised up in order to keep us from humanizing the mysteries of God.

In a separate chapter we shall speak of the Eucharistic sacrifice as being officially the act of a people. The Eucharist as the spiritual nutriment of the soul interests us here. The manna of the Jewish people was truly the badge of a whole people; for forty years a nation grew up on it. This power of building up the new people of God is, of course, incomprehensibly greater in the case of the Eucharist. But let us bear well in mind that it is useless to approach dogmatically this great mystery of the divine Bread unless we start with the assumption that in its institution Christ thought, not of individuals, but of a people.

The hesitations which have been noticeable amongst Catholics at certain periods relative to the measure of distribution of the Bread of life, the holy Eucharist, have had their counterpart in that other sacrament whose very nature it is to deal with the common people—the sacrament of Penance. As this sacrament is administered today by the Catholic Church, it breaks the record of every kind of institution for its unlimited and illimitable popularity. Is there anything like the Catholic confessional to give an impression of a people that has the consciousness of its own life? The practice of this sacrament supposes a God who looks after the least of His people and who does not wish anyone to be lost. In the Gospel of St. Matthew our Lord ends the parable of the lost sheep over whose return there is more rejoicing than over the ninety-nine, with the significant words:

> Even so it is not the will of your Father who is in heaven, that one of these little ones should perish (Matt 18:14).

As with Baptism and with the Eucharist this sacrament is announced in terms of the greatest comprehensiveness. On the day of His resurrection from the dead, the Son of God spoke the words that embrace the whole world:

> When he had said this, he breathed on them; and he said to them: Receive ye the Holy Ghost. Whose sins you shall forgive, they are forgiven them: and whose sins you shall retain, they are retained (John 20:22-23).

Christ does not expect His people to be sinless; the conditions of human existence are against such a totality of purity. He takes it for granted that His people will sin much at times, but for those sad blemishes they will not cease to be His people. So He has placed in the midst of them the stream of pure water, the sacrament in which all the races that compose His people will wash their garments.

Catholicism believes in this great power of the Keys, the power that can absolve from their sins innumerable multitudes of men, can sanctify them and render them acceptable to the eyes of God. Only tentatively was the immensity of this power realized by some. There was always the dread lest the mercy of God be made valueless and common. Penitents were considered as a class apart, as condemned criminals are a class apart in the natural state. But the full understanding of this sacrament, just as in the case of the Bread of Life, came when Christians had become a great and numerous people, when the law of sacramental life became essentially the law of the multitudes.

There have always been men who have made it their task to deride what they call the materialism of the Catholic Church, the faith of that Church in the powers of elemental signs. They have poured torrents of scorn on this primitive religious mentality, as they call it; they have even pronounced the word "magic," as if the sacramental faith of the Church were only another form of the ancient superstitions and incantations. This sort of religious superiority is, of course, a very cheap form of self-deceit; a man is not nearer to God because he has nothing but contempt for the fringe of God's garment—the material world. But leaving alone the psychological depravity which is the source of that kind of spiritual pride, contempt for the Church's sacramental faith can be found there only where there is ignorance of the true conditions of the super natural vocation in Christ. "I did not come to call the just but the sinners," may have been on the lips of Christ an ironical remark for the benefit of the Pharisees who thought themselves to be just men not in need of any call to another life. But Christ's mission without any doubt is this: to call to the highest life a very sinful and a very degraded world, a world sick in body and in soul.

That there should be the "oil of the sick," *oleum infirmorum*, as a divine institution on a par with the Eucharist, is of course a marvelous thought but not a surprising one. Water, wine and oil become irresistible powers of sanctification in the hands of the Word Incarnate. The oil of the sick is the medicine of the people of God; it heals, or at least, it softens the wound of death, it gives the people of God comfort in the last hour. Not an elaborate ritual, not a heroic attitude, not a mental transport is expected from the Christian when he is sick unto death, when he is on the point of departing this life; all that is asked of him is this, that he should send for the priest who will anoint him with the holy oil and who will pronounce over him the "prayer of faith." It is thus that the people of God pass away in the power of God, uplifted through a divine institution, a sacrament which is within the reach of the poorest and the simplest.

There is in this last sacrament a divine aroma which puts one in mind of the words of Christ when Mary "anointed the feet of Jesus" and wiped His feet with her hair, and the house was filled with the odor of the ointment, and the Lord said, "Let her alone, that she may keep it against the day of my burial" (John 12:7). Every one of the people of God is entitled to the supreme honor of being anointed with the oil of sanctification; he leaves this world not burdened but refreshed, not saddened but gladdened; the terror of death is not upon the people of God; on the contrary, death and burial are functions of grace and mercy.

It has been truly said that all historic nations show their special character in those rites that surround the dying and the dead, in fact, the tombs of ancient nations are the most authentic records of their history; nationhood and death have never been separated except in modern, materialistic society. The people of God have a ritual of death which is all their own, which alone would suffice to distinguish them from every other people the world has ever known.

✠ 15 ✠

THE PEOPLE OF GOD AND THE ALTAR

No FEATURE IN THE LIFE AND FORTUNES OF THE ancient people of God had greater saliency than the existence in its midst of the altar of God. The altar was the pivot of its nationhood. Political rebellions always meant that another altar had been erected against the altar that was in the Temple at Jerusalem. When Jeroboam set out to separate, finally, his portion of the Jewish people from the legitimate king at Jerusalem, he built for the ten tribes two altars, one in Bethel and the other in Dan. But this outrage to the oneness of God's worship in Israel was denounced at once, and terrible vengeances were prophesied without delay:

> And behold there came a man of God out of Judah, by the word of the Lord to Bethel, when Jeroboam was standing upon the altar, and burning incense. And he cried out against the altar in the word of the Lord, and said: O Altar, Altar, thus saith the Lord: Behold a child shall be born to the house of David, Josiah

by name. And he shall immolate upon thee the priests of the high places, who now burn incense upon thee: and he shall burn men's bones upon thee (1 Kings 13:1-2).

The offering up of the daily sacrifices was the most manifest sign of national continuance and the cessation of the sacrifices was identical with national dissolution:

> And after sixty-two weeks Christ shall be slain: and the people that deny him shall not be his. And a people, with their leader that shall come, shall destroy the city and the sanctuary: and the end thereof shall be waste, and after the end of the war the appointed desolation. And he shall confirm the covenant with many, in one week: and in the half of the week the victim and the sacrifice shall fail: and there shall be in the temple the abomination of desolation. And the desolation shall continue even to the consummation and to the end (Dan 9:26-27).

One might as well attempt to write the history of Rome without mentioning Rome's wars as to write the history of Israel without the preponderant role of the altar of God in its midst.

There is in all this awe before the altar an extreme simplicity of outlook. St. Paul, who was brought up in the religion of the Jewish altar, puts it thus in his first Epistle to the Corinthians:

> Behold Israel according to the flesh. Are not they that eat of the sacrifices partakers of the altar (1 Cor 10:18)?

The devout Jew brings to the altar the victim that he intends for God. The priest immolates it officially. The man who brings the victim, with his family, eats a portion of the hallowed flesh of the animal; through this banquet they all become partakers of the altar, they share its religion, its nobility, its power of propitiation. They are truly a people of the altar. Theocracy is embodied in the rite of the altar. Every Jewish child can be made to understand this simple theology of the sacrifice.

But great as is the historic evidence concerning the place which the altar held in Jewish nationalism, the history of the altar in the new people of God, in Christendom, makes the ancient altar-lore pale into a mere shadow, into a simple figure of that which was to come. The history of the Catholic altar is written on the surface of the Christian world in true monumental fashion. Those portions of the globe which Christianity has conquered are studded with the stones of altars, as if they had been scattered all over the planet through some mighty flood of grace, as geologists attribute to the invasion of ice and water the presence of innumerable rocks and boulders on the face of the earth. People may say that it was a rank error, a superstition, a blasphemous fable to hold that a sacrifice could be offered up by Christians. But one thing no man in his senses can deny is the existence of these altars without number. The people of God of the new Covenant are more radically and more universally a people of the altar than were the Jews.

Nor need we appeal exclusively to the past in order to establish this preponderance of the altar mentality in the people of God. Today, as much as ever, the mystical smoke of the divine Sacrifice ascends from thousands of altars from one end of the globe to the other. The destruction of the altar by the so-called "New Learning," the Protestant Reformation, has not been more than the damage done by a winter gale amongst the trees of a forest; even if there are permanent treeless patches in the woods to mark forever the fury of the tempest, the forest still stands and there is much new growth even in the places of devastation. Thus today there are thousands of altars in this England of ours which at one time was swept by an anti-altar heresy. As for the past, Europe's religious, artistic and even economic history centers round the altar where the Sacrifice of the Mass was offered up. I make so bold as to connect the European economics of bygone ages with the altar because, as any reader of history knows, an enormous percentage of landed property was dedicated to the service of the altar in one way or another.

So vast is the history of the Catholic altar that no one could write it without at the same time giving full and detailed accounts of the lives and doings of a hundred generations of Christians. Not a public deed, not a private act of religion, not a nuptial contract was there without the altar. Everything took place in front of the altar; from the altar the Emperors received their crowns, the knights their swords, the consecrated virgins their veils; on the altar the monk laid the parchment that recorded his profession; in front of the altar all Christians have been married at all times. The Jewish altar was one for a whole nation, the Christian altar is also one in mystery but innumerable in material presence; in other words, the one divine Sacrifice of the Eucharist is celebrated in every spot of the globe wherever a few of the faithful are gathered round a consecrated priest. There never has been, there could not be, another people whose fortunes are so irretrievably entwined round the altar.

This omnipresence of the altar among the people of God would alone be sufficient to stamp that people as a class of men entirely unique. It may be conceded that the Hellenistic and the Roman religions had a great sense for the importance of the altar, that they multiplied altars with great profusion; but even apart from the abysmal difference of the faith—one being, as St. Paul puts it, the table of the devils, the other the table of the Lord—the Christians who succeeded the Greeks and the Romans even in matters of numbers were immensely more lavish with their altars.

It is therefore to be taken for granted that the whole concept of the people of God as expounded in this book is profoundly modified by the theology of the Christian altar, so that we are justified in saying that for the Christian, even more than for the Jew, spiritual nationhood and altar are interchangeable terms. There can be no people of God where there is no altar. As long as men gather round the altar, believe in the altar, keep the altar erect, their divine nationhood remains immune. It may be that the rites of the altar, the Sacrifice of the Mass, are condemned by the public authorities, by the dark powers that are in command, but, if it is possible for a priest to find a cave or a garret in which to celebrate Mass, the constitutional issues of the people of God remain unchanged: where there is an altar there is the people of God.

The dogmatic implications of the Christian altar are, of course, infinitely more profound than was the Jewish view of the daily sacrifice. The Israelite viewed his victim as a gift unto God; so does the Christian, but with this far-reaching difference, that the gift is not an earthly thing but a divine reality, the Son of God Himself, in the state of oblation. In the Eucharistic Sacrifice we offer up to God directly, in virtue of the words that are spoken at the altar, the Body and the Blood of God's beloved Son.

In the whole creation there could be nothing holier than these two realities, the Body of the Son of God and the Blood of the Son of God. But the incomprehensible wealth in the Thing offered up ought in no wise to hinder the Christian from a very simple attitude when he is standing before the altar. He knows, through his faith, that under the appearance of bread and wine there is offered up to God the Body and the Blood of the Son of God: for him this is not only part of the truth but the whole truth; it expresses all the characteristics of that divine transaction. He knows that once upon a time, on Mount Calvary, the Son of God shed His Blood; that His Blood was separated from His Flesh; this was the supreme Sacrifice which redeemed the whole World. On the Christian altar the same mystery takes place under the appearance of bread and wine, but without any of the horrors and the sufferings of Calvary.

This view is infinitely simple though infinitely deep. The Christian is truly not asked to make an effort of intellectual comprehension greater than was the mental outlook of the Jew at his sacrifice; his faith indeed is greater, because he accepts a higher mystery, but he accepts that mystery with as much simplicity as the Israelite accepted the validity of his sacrifice. It is a gift to God of what is most excellent in heaven and on earth: the living Flesh and the living Blood of the Word Incarnate. Not that the theology of the Sacrifice stops there; it has further regions for the mystically-minded to explore, but this the ordinary Christian need not do. For him the letter of the Sacrifice is all he needs, for in that letter the whole mystery of God is contained:

> This is my Body, this is my Blood, which is poured out for you, and for many, unto the remission of sins.

It is, of course, obvious to everyone that men who in the sincerity of their faith enter into participation with this mystery of the Catholic altar belong to another world, to the unseen world where God is the supreme ruler, where the rights and claims of God hold sovereign sway. In our own days we are not without experience of human societies to whom all the ideals embodied in the doctrine of the altar are an abomination. Every day brings out more vividly the abysmal difference of outlook between men who believe in an altar and men who destroy that altar. It may be remarked in extenuation of what has been said just now that orthodox Protestantism has kept at least this much, it believes in the altar of the Cross, though it denies the sacramental altar of the Catholic Church; but the total denial of the altar is found to breed a human race which very soon will have nothing in common with the ancient Christian civilization except the lands in which that civilization flourished.

It is of importance, therefore, that the Catholic people be left in its simplicity of faith with regard to that mystery of the altar. Every child, with the grace of Baptism, is a participant of the altar; all that is beautiful, all that is attractive, ought to be pressed into the service of the altar. No pains ought to be spared to enable the Christian people to approach the altar. Let us be quite convinced that the simple fact of the Catholic people attending Mass once a week is an immense spiritual gain. It is a roll-call of God. It is a weekly census of the people of God.

Though it be a laudable thing to teach the Catholic multitudes how to enter more deeply into the mystery of the Mass through personal devotion and attention, it would, on the other hand, be a mistaken policy to exact too intense a degree of individual piety, as if the Mass were nothing else than a good occasion for self-improvement. Mass is this and more; but above all things it is the rallying of the people of God; it is a divine act, done independently of the people; a proclamation of God's sovereignty, to which the multitudes of the faithful are expected to shout their approval.

There is really nothing like the Eucharistic Sacrifice in the whole range of human activities, natural and spiritual. As already frequently insinuated, the only valid analogy is the sacrificial economy of the ancient Law. The Christian altar is the place where God does His most independent work, independent of human merit and human co-operation; it is a divine fire which burns in virtue of its own inner force and all that man can do or need do is to come within the radius of the heat of that fire.

Many are scandalized at this proclamation of the transcending gratuity of the effects of the Eucharistic Sacrifice; they seem to fear lest man should obtain his salvation too cheaply. But all we know, and we know a vast deal concerning the gratuitousness of the gifts of God, is true in a thousand-fold way in this matter of the Christian altar. A whole people in its millions is given by God this power to glorify Him, to appease Him, to protest their loyalty to Him, to present their petitions to Him, in a sacrifice absolutely worthy of Him.

✠ 16 ✠

The Consecration of the People

The meaning of the word laicism is known to everyone: it stands for that terrible modern tendency to deny any kind of supernatural consecration, both in the case of individual man and of institutions. That other term, secularism, expresses the same unfortunate exclusion of idealisms. A State that recognizes no priesthood, no sanctification of men and women, no holiness of days and places, is a State in which laicism is supreme.

The secularist also abominates the notion of any supernatural privilege. If a thing could be defined by its contraries, the notion of the people of God becomes clear to us if we call it the very opposite of laicism and secularism. The people of God abounds in consecrations of every sort, it abounds in supernatural privilege, in special vocations and higher calls; there is no member of that people who is not the subject of some consecration, who cannot aspire to further and higher consecrations. In other words, there are no layman in the people of God, taking now the term laymen to mean one who is untouched by some supernatural unction, the whole people of God are anointed in the Spirit of God that dwells in them.

Laicism and secularism, then, are the total denial of the supernatural whilst the people of God are its very embodiment. St. Paul's enumeration of the spiritual gifts is applicable in its entirety to this great people as all Christians are spiritual men: there is not in the people of God, one section that has the gifts of the Spirit and another section that is devoid of them, being left, so to speak, to mere natural resources; the Spirit animates the whole people. There is a diversity of gifts but there is oneness of consecration:

> For in one Spirit were we all baptized into one body, whether Jews or Gentiles, whether bond or free: and in one Spirit we have all been made to drink (1 Cor 12:13).

This text of St. Paul is illuminating precisely from this point of view, that it does not allude to a hierarchy of specially ordained men, but to the common mass of Christians, where the Jew and the Gentile, the slave and the freeman, rub shoulders. Quite simply then the multitudes of the Christian people have drunk of one and the same Spirit, the Holy Ghost, who came down on Pentecost to abide forever with the people. The people of God is what it is through the Spirit dwelling in the midst of it, and that Spirit manifests His presence through innumerable powers and gifts which enable that race of the elect to perform the deeds of life.

The Holy Ghost is the bond of union between all the citizens of that higher nation; through Him they are made into one consecrated society, they have all drunk of Him as of an elixir of life, and His vitalities run in their veins forever. No one ought to attempt to describe the people of God without presupposing this communion of all the members of that people in the one divine Spirit, the Holy Ghost. He is truly their blood, He is their racial psychology, He is the source of all their fervors; but, being One, He manifests Himself in a variety of gifts and powers.

The secularist has done enormous harm in the world; very few of us are able to gauge the depth of the apostasy that has taken place in European society since the process of laicization started some two hundred years ago. We all know that laicism is an entirely Western phenomenon; the Eastern races before they are contaminated by Western civilization abominate secularism nearly as much as does the Catholic Church, for none of those races would condescend to consider themselves as unprivileged, at least in some vague and pantheistic form.

This hatred of privilege which has come over the Western world is extolled by men in their blindness as being a sign of a free spirit and of advanced thought. But let us be quite clear on this subject: privilege is the very essence of the people of God. That people is what it is because it is not left to its merely natural resources; there is not a child in the people of God who does not find itself raised above itself and placed in relative spiritual security. Enemies there are to endanger that security, but this does not prevent the providence of predilection from being the dominant factor in every member of the people of God.

Priesthood is, of course, the first object of assault on the part of the laicist, we mean now the official hieratic priesthood whose functions are even more privileged than the ordinary activities of the people of God. We may take it for granted that the priesthood in the new people of God could have possessed a variety of forms. We know how in the ancient people it was propagated through the family of Levi.

No such caste limitation was to be found in the new people of God. Every man has it in himself to become a priest through the initial sanctification of Baptism, because the people itself, in its totality, is God's inheritance; its initial consecrations are of so high an order that the further or more specified consecrations of Holy Orders do not establish a chasm between the priesthood and the people, but from amongst the whole people God chooses the ministers of the altar. Nothing could bring out more evidently the fundamental excellence of the people of God than this universality of a possible vocation; that all men, from all ranks, are radically capable of receiving the highest forms of dedication to God's service.

One of the commonest forms of misunderstanding of Catholic things on the part of non-Catholics is this, that the non-Catholic almost without exception thinks of the Catholic priesthood as a class of men who lord it over their fellow-Christians, as a powerful political caste would make itself felt on those less privileged. A more disastrous caricature of Catholic life there could hardly be. Nothing is more contrary to the whole genius of the people of God than such a difference between the priest and the ordinary Catholic. The very fact we have described of that universal consecration of the people of God through the Holy Ghost renders impossible such a hiatus in conditions, and at no time has there been, between the Catholic priest and the people, that chasm which has existed and does exist in the secular state between the classes that govern and the classes that are governed. In the people of God it can never be more than a variety of gifts, not a division into those that are endowed and those that are not endowed with the charismata of the Spirit; for all are without doubt endowed.

The boldest act of faith on the part of the people of God in the possibilities of super natural consecration is found in the view taken by that people of the sanctity of marriage. That matrimony should be a sacrament in the eyes of Catholic generations is certainly a triumph of human idealism. Nor can it be said that such a faith is not operative, is not practical. It shows its grasp on reality through the very fact of its indissolubility. A people that submits to the belief that all union in wedlock is indissoluble, because it is a tie made, not by the hand of man, but by the hand of God, has achieved a degree of racial mysticism for which there is no parallel in the history of the world. The people of God have never committed the sin of unbelief in God's right to order their lives.

To anyone who reflects, this universal acceptance by the Catholic of all times of the divine ruling that matrimony is a sacrament and therefore indissoluble, is an achievement in the spiritual world so great that by itself it can be quoted as a testimony of the divine characteristics of the religion which is the religion of the people of God.

But indissolubility is not the only sacredness of the Christian marriage. Matrimonial life itself is a consecrated state because it is the normal way of propagation for the people of God:

> For the unbelieving husband is sanctified by the believing wife: and the unbelieving wife is sanctified by the believing husband. Otherwise your children would be unclean: but now they are holy (1 Cor 7:14).

Even in the case when only one of the two partners is a Christian, according to St. Paul, there is already a sanctification. The holiness here predicated of the children must not be thought to be the same thing as the sanctity received in baptism: it is enough if we give to these words the interpretation that in virtue of the Christian's marriage, even with an infidel, there is a strict right for the offspring to be grafted on to the mystical Body of Christ by baptism. This right in itself constitutes a holiness. The source of all human corruption, sexual intercourse, is truly consecrated by Christ, is made to be a participation in the divine vitalities of the Word of God through whom all things were made.

Conclusion

St. Ambrose gives a definition of the Church which is as beautiful as it is unusual:

Ex duobus igitur constat Ecclesia: ut aut peccare nesciat, aut peccare desinat.

The Church is made up of two perfections: it either knows not sin or it relinquishes sin.[7]

Sinlessness and repentance for sin committed, such is the Church's sanctity here on earth, and such is the perfection we have to expect from the people of God.

The Liturgy of the Church abounds in that wisdom, it unceasingly speaks of a holy people, but also of a people that is everlastingly in need of purification. In the Canon of the Mass the Christian multitudes are described as the slaves of God, but also as God's holy people:

Unde et memores, Domine, nos servi tui, sed et plebs tua sancta.

---

7 Lib. 7, in Luc., c. II.

Innumerable are the prayers in the official Latin liturgy in which Christians are proclaimed to be the people of God. There is a matchless music for the spiritually-minded in the ever-recurring words: *populus Tuus Domine* ("your people, oh Lord").

But not only prayer, action also is intimately associated with this perennial title; could one not suggest that the theology of the "people of God" would be most helpful towards a broader understanding of the claims of the "Catholic action"? Without any doubt the underlying thought of the latter is an objection to that specialization of work by ecclesiastics themselves. It is positively wrong to identify God's service with ritual or sacramental functions; a whole people must serve God with a variety of endowments truly unlimited. If the Church is not only a supernatural institution but, as we have tried to show in this book, a "people of God," it ought to be evident that not one man is really outside the scheme of active cooperation in the realization of God's plan.

Secularization of human life is a great evil and an immense error, but it would also be an error, not to say an evil, to give the Christian life an exclusively ecclesiastical meaning, as if the ecclesiastical life alone were the true Christian life: it is only one form of that life. To take away from the Christian people the notion and the sentiment of universal consecration would be a disastrous procedure; to think of them, on the other hand, in terms of a "people of God" is, we hope a formula which is not only wonderfully consoling, but also in practice most operative and useful. A divine people is never inactive; it has a holy ambition, it aspires to the establishment of the kingdom of God.

THE END

www.ingramcontent.com/pod-product-compliance
Lightning Source LLC
Chambersburg PA
CBHW020006050426
42450CB00005B/336